EXTRAORDINARY RECIPES FROM

FLORIDA KEYS &
KEY WEST CHEF'S TABLE

VICTORIA SHEARER

Photography by Michael Marrero

THE CONCH REPUBLIC

Guilford, Connecticut

Globe Pequot is an imprint of Rowman & Littlefield

Distributed by NATIONAL BOOK NETWORK

Copyright © 2014 by Rowman & Littlefield

Photography by Michael Marrero, except image on pages 100–101 © Licensed by Shutterstock.com

British Library Cataloguing in Publication Information Available

Library of Congress Cataloging-in-Publication Data

Shearer, Victoria.
  Florida Keys & Key West chef's table : extraordinary recipes from the Conch Republic / Victoria Shearer ; photography by Michael Marrero.
      pages cm — (Chef's table)
  Includes index.
  ISBN 978-0-7627-9458-4 (hardback)
  1. Cooking, American—Southern style. 2. Cooking—Florida—Key West. 3. Cooking, Caribbean. I. Title. II. Title: Florida Keys and Key West chef's table.
  TX715.2.S68S4949 2014
  641.5975—dc23
                                        2014027542

♾ The paper used in this publication meets the minimum requirements of American National Standard for Information Sciences—Permanence of Paper for Printed Library Materials, ANSI/NISO Z39.48-1992.

Restaurants and chefs often come and go, and menus are ever changing. We recommend you call ahead to obtain current information before visiting any of the establishments in this book.

For Bob, who has made my life's journey
such an incredible ride.

Contents

RECIPES BY COURSE xiii

ACKNOWLEDGMENTS. xvii

INTRODUCTION 1

THE FLORIDA KEYS

The Fish House 6
Pasta with Shrimp & Cilantro-Lime Pesto
Shrimp Bundles with Basil & Prosciutto

The Fish House Encore. 10
Fish Flagler
Encore Pumpkin Bisque with Crabmeat

Key Largo Conch House 13
Lobster Bisque

Snook's Bayside 16
Pistachio-Encrusted Yellowtail Snapper with Sweet Chili Sauce
Hazelnut Chicken

Key Largo Fisheries 20
Dottie's Key Largo Smoked Fish Dip

M.E.A.T. 22
M.E.A.T.'s Signature Ketchup
Inside-Out Juicy Lucy Burger

Robert Is Here Fruit Stand 26
Canistel Strawberry Shake

Ziggie & Mad Dog's 28
Smothered Tenderloin Medallions
White Truffle Lobster Mac & Cheese

ATLANTIC'S EDGE 32
Hogfish à la Plancha

KAIYO GRILL 36
Yellowtail Tiradito

PIERRE'S AT MORADA BAY 38
Grilled Octopus with Crispy Capers, Extra-Virgin Olive Oil, Smoked Paprika & Green Pea Tendrils
Local Hogfish Meunière with Olive Oil Poached Potatoes, Haricots Verts, and Heirloom Tomato
    & Parsley Salad

MORADA BAY BEACH CAFE 43
Whole Fried Snapper with Tropical Sweet Chili Salsa & Warm Vegetable Slaw

ISLAMORADA FISH COMPANY 46
Fresh Catch-of-the-Day with Shrimp Portofino Sauce

SUNKEN TREASURE—STONE CRAB CLAWS 49

GREEN TURTLE INN 50
Shrimp Sliders
Lobster-Stuffed Squash Blossom Salad

SPANISH GARDENS CAFE 54
Salmorejo with Shrimp, Avocado & Serrano Ham
Chocolate Valencia

LAZY DAYS 58
Hogfish Tropical

DOLPHIN BISTRO 62
Key Lime Parfait
Miso Braised Pork Belly & Key Lime–Chili Seared Sea Scallops over Risotto

PLAZA GRILL 66
Whole Roasted Yellowtail with Asian Vegetables, Jasmine Rice & Ginger Soy Vinaigrette

BARRACUDA GRILL 69
Pan-Seared Scallops Served over Pesto Pasta
Voodoo Seafood Stew

KEYS FISHERIES MARKET & MARINA 72

Sautéed Lobster Tails

CASTAWAY WATERFRONT RESTAURANT & SUSHI BAR 75

Castaway's Wreck Diver-Style Lionfish

Beef Yu-Ke (Asian Raw Beef Salad)

NO NAME PUB 79

Royal Pub Pizza

Spicy Pub Conch Fritters

STAR ATTRACTION—KEY LIME PIE 84

Mattie's Key Lime Pie

THE DINING ROOM AT LITTLE PALM ISLAND 86

Lobster with Roasted Corn & Apple Risotto

Tequila Ceviche Little Palm Island

Square Grouper Bar & Grill 91

Toasted Almond-Encrusted Grouper with Warm Caribbean Pineapple Relish

Island Shrimp Cakes with Island Pepper Aioli

Kaya Island Eats 96

Pacific Rim Tuna Poke

Rasta Pasta with Macadamia Nut Jerk Pesto

KEY WEST

Azur Restaurant 102

Caramelized Brussels Sprouts with Pancetta & Pecorino Romano

Roesti Benedict

Banana Cafe 106

Yellowtail Snapper in Citrus Sauce

Tuna Tartare

Better Than Sex, A Dessert Restaurant 112

Sex Addict

Conch Republic Seafood Company 115

Blackened Scallops with Risotto-Style Israeli Couscous

Key West Pink Shrimp with Vera Cruz Sauce

Stormy Waters

KEY WEST HISTORIC BAR CRAWL 120

SLOPPY JOE'S BAR 120

Sloppy Joe's Mojito

SCHOONER WHARF BAR 121

Frozen Mango Mint Margarita

GREEN PARROT BAR 122

Green Parrot Root Beer Barrel

HOG'S BREATH SALOON 123

World Famous Hog's Breath Saloon Key Lime Shooter

Cuban Coffee Queen 124
Cuban Mix Sandwich

Garbo's Grill 127
Korean Bulgogi Tacos

Glazed Donuts 130
Roasted Pineapple Brûlée Donuts

Half Shell Raw Bar 134
Red Conch Chowder

Where the Sun Sinks into the Sea—Sunset Pier 136
Cuban Pork Empanadas with Guava Barbecue Sauce
Sunset Pier's Pusser's Painkiller

Hot Tin Roof 140
Coconut Chorizo Stew Topped with Grilled Grouper
Hot Tin Huevos Rancheros

Latitudes Restaurant 144
Sweet Potato Crusted Grouper with Truffle Cauliflower Puree and Roasted Garlic
     & Thyme Cream Sauce
Butter Poached Florida Lobster Tail with Creamy Herb Polenta, Champagne Beurre Blanc,
     Caviar & Asparagus

Louie's Backyard 150
Grilled Lamb Rib Chops with Cauliflower-Chèvre Puree & Sun-dried Tomato Relish
Chocolate Brownie Crème Brûlée

Martin's Restaurant 154
Grouper Dijon over Champagne Sauerkraut

Michaels Restaurant 157
Scallops & Brie with Ruby Port Reduction
Key Lime Martini

New York Pasta Garden 161
Seafood Lasagna Trescaline

Nine One Five..164

Moroccan Lamb Loin with Vegetable Tagine

Crab Cakes with Fingerling Potatoes, Andouille Sausage, Artichokes & Lemon Aioli

key west master chef's classic...........................168

Old Town Bakery.......................................170

Gorgonzola-Walnut Baguettes

Lemon Honey Pound Cake

One Duval at Pier House Resort & Spa..............174

Sautéed Gulf Shrimp with Smoked Bacon & Cremini Mushroom Beurre Blanc

Crab & Avocado Timbale

Prime 951 Steakhouse..................................178

Double Bone Pork Chop with Mushroom Cabernet Sauce

Roof Top Cafe..180

Duck Tostados

Seared Sea Scallops with Edamame, Roasted Shiitakes & Sherry Miso Butter

Santiago's Bodega.....................................184

Yellowfin Tuna Ceviche

Korean-Style Short Ribs with Cherry-Hoisin Glaze & Orange-Miso Slaw

Square One...188

Shrimp & Grits

Pirate's Pie

advice from a chef's kitchen...........................192

Strip House Key West..................................193

The Perfect Steak

Truffle Creamed Spinach

Turtle Kraals...198

Ropa Vieja

Nikkei Ceviche

Index..202

About the Author & Photographer.....................206

Recipes by Course

SOUPS, CHOWDERS & STEWS

Lobster Bisque. 14
Encore Pumpkin Bisque with Crabmeat 12
Red Conch Chowder. 135
Salmorejo with Shrimp, Avocado & Serrano Ham 56
Voodoo Seafood Stew. 71

SMALL PLATES, SALADS, STARTERS & SIDES

Beef Yu-Ke (Asian Raw Beef Salad). 77
Caramelized Brussels Sprouts with Pancetta & Pecorino Romano 103
Crab & Avocado Timbale. 177
Crab Cakes with Fingerling Potatoes, Andouille Sausage, Artichokes & Lemon Aioli 166
Cuban Pork Empanadas with Guava Barbecue Sauce 138
Dottie's Key Largo Smoked Fish Dip 21
Duck Tostados. 181
Gorgonzola-Walnut Baguettes. 171
Grilled Octopus with Crispy Capers, Extra-Virgin Olive Oil, Smoked Paprika & Green Pea Tendrils. 40
Island Shrimp Cakes with Island Pepper Aioli 94
Lobster-Stuffed Squash Blossom Salad 52
M.E.A.T.'s Signature Ketchup 23
Nikkei Ceviche 200
Pacific Rim Tuna Poke 97
Scallops & Brie with Ruby Port Reduction. 159
Shrimp Bundles with Basil & Prosciutto. 9
Shrimp Sliders 51
Spicy Pub Conch Fritters. 82
Tequila Ceviche Little Palm Island 90
Truffle Creamed Spinach 196
Tuna Tartare. 110
White Truffle Lobster Mac & Cheese 31
Yellowfin Tuna Ceviche. 185

Blackened Scallops with Risotto-Style Israeli Couscous 116

Butter Poached Florida Lobster Tail with Creamy Herb Polenta, Champagne Beurre Blanc,
   Caviar & Asparagus 148

Castaway's Wreck Diver-Style Lionfish 76

Coconut Chorizo Stew Topped with Grilled Grouper 142

Cuban Mix Sandwich 125

Double Bone Pork Chop with Mushroom Cabernet Sauce 179

Fish Flagler 11

Fresh Catch-of-the-Day with Shrimp Portofino Sauce 48

Grilled Lamb Rib Chops with Cauliflower-Chèvre Puree & Sun-dried Tomato Relish 151

Grouper Dijon over Champagne Sauerkraut 155

Hazelnut Chicken 18

Hogfish à la Plancha 34

Hogfish Tropical 60

Hot Tin Huevos Rancheros 143

Inside-Out Juicy Lucy Burger 24

Key West Pink Shrimp with Vera Cruz Sauce 119

Korean Bulgogi Tacos 128

Korean-Style Short Ribs with Cherry-Hoisin Glaze & Orange-Miso Slaw 187

Lobster with Roasted Corn & Apple Risotto 88

Local Hogfish Meunière with Olive Oil Poached Potatoes, Haricots Verts & Heirloom Tomato
   & Parsley Salad 41

Miso Braised Pork Belly & Key Lime–Chili Seared Sea Scallops over Risotto 64

Moroccan Lamb Loin with Vegetable Tagine 165

Pan-Seared Scallops Served over Pesto Pasta 70

Pasta with Shrimp & Cilantro-Lime Pesto 8

The Perfect Steak 195

Pistachio-Encrusted Yellowtail Snapper with Sweet Chili Sauce 17

Rasta Pasta with Macadamia Nut Jerk Pesto 98

Roesti Benedict 105

Ropa Vieja 199

Royal Pub Pizza 81

Sautéed Gulf Shrimp with Smoked Bacon & Cremini Mushroom Beurre Blanc 175

Sautéed Lobster Tails 74

Seafood Lasagna Trescaline 162

Seared Sea Scallops with Edamame, Roasted Shiitakes & Sherry Miso Butter 183

Shrimp & Grits 189

Smothered Tenderloin Medallions 29

Sweet Potato Crusted Grouper with Truffle Cauliflower Puree and Roasted Garlic & Thyme Cream Sauce . . 146
Toasted Almond-Encrusted Grouper with Warm Caribbean Pineapple Relish. 92
Whole Fried Snapper with Tropical Sweet Chili Salsa & Warm Vegetable Slaw 45
Whole Roasted Yellowtail with Asian Vegetables, Jasmine Rice & Ginger Soy Vinaigrette. 67
Yellowtail Snapper in Citrus Sauce 107
Yellowtail Tiradito 37

Sweets

Chocolate Brownie Crème Brûlée 153
Chocolate Valencia 57
Key Lime Parfait. 63
Lemon Honey Pound Cake 173
Manny & Isa's Key Lime Pie 85
Pirate's Pie. 191
Roasted Pineapple Brûlée Donuts. 132
Sex Addict 113

Beverages

Canistel Strawberry Shake. 27
Frozen Mango Mint Margarita 121
Green Parrot Root Beer Barrel. 122
Key Lime Martini 160
Sloppy Joe's Mojito 120
Stormy Waters. 119
Sunset Pier's Pusser's Painkiller 139
World Famous Hog's Breath Saloon Key Lime Shooter. 123

Acknowledgments

This has been such an amazing yearlong project. Stepping out of my kitchen and into the lives of the Florida Keys' best chefs opened a window that gave me a brief glimpse of what goes on beyond the menus, behind the kitchen doors, and in the minds of this very special breed of artists. I feel as if I made a cadre of new friends, and, for sure, I gained insight and a heightened appreciation for the passion, dedication, and, yes, sacrifice these talented men and women bring to the table.

I send my undying gratitude to the chefs, owners, and managers of the restaurants and drinking establishments featured in this book for taking the time to create and contribute special recipes, for following through with the paperwork and e-mails amid your very busy, crazy schedules, for so candidly sharing your stories with me in our interviews, and for opening your establishments for photo shoots.

My thanks as well to the public relations firms' representatives, who liaised with their client chefs on my behalf, chased down recipes, and set up interviews and photo shoots. Your constant good humor and timely communications were very welcome.

Thank you to Robert Moehling of Robert Is Here for allowing us to feature his famous fruit stand—my favorite—in the book. A very special thank you as well to Gordon Ross of MARC for inviting me to be a judge at his fantastic Key West Master Chef's Classic challenge. I had a ball! And the food . . . oh, the food! And to Chef Carl Stanton, instructor for Marathon High School's culinary program, thank you for allowing your students to be a part of this project.

To Amy Lyons at Globe Pequot Press, who once again has offered me the opportunity to write a fascinating new book, thank you. It has been a labor of love. My gratitude as well to Mike Marrero, the fantastic Key West photographer who brought this book to life with his amazing images.

Thank you to my husband, Bob, for his constant and undying support of my crazy writing projects, for "suffering" through the winter months in the Keys by fishing while I was interviewing chefs, and for understanding the "shhhhh!" when I was writing.

And, I send a shout-out to my children, my grandchildren, and my loyal friends, who understood and forgave as I all but abandoned them in the run-up to my book deadline. "Here she goes again," they say.

Like most of the chefs of the Florida Keys, I "washed ashore," too, back in the early nineties. I discovered then that the islands have a flavor all their own, that there is no place quite like it in the United States . . . on Earth, maybe. We call our special corner of the world Paradise. Savor the tastes of the Florida Keys!

Introduction

Life on a Rock

The Florida Keys rose from the sea—a string of patch reefs—after the last glacial period, the Wisconsin. Unique in the United States, 1,700 islands comprise the archipelago, but only 43 are connected by bridges and inhabited. Straddling the Atlantic Ocean and the Gulf of Mexico, this chain of pearls—known locally as Paradise—enjoys a tropical climate, copious sunshine, and bountiful piscatorial resources.

The seafaring Calusas, Tequestas, and Matecumbes maintained tribal cultures here as early as AD 800, as witnessed by mounds of bones and shells found in kitchen middens that suggested fish, crabs, sea turtles, lobsters, shellfish, and conchs were plentiful. By the 1600s conquistadors and pirates had invaded nearby waters, with Spain capturing Cuba and Florida, and England colonizing the Bahamas. Control of the territories bounced back and forth between the two countries for centuries, but neither country colonized the Keys, deeming them uninhabitable.

The Bahamians and Cubans did, however, regularly harvest Keys waters. Cuban fishermen referred to the islands as *los cayos de Florida*, the little islands of Florida. The Bahamians adopted the word *cayo* and changed it to "cay." Eventually the word was corrupted to "key," and by 1742 the English were calling the islands the Florida Keys.

Spain ceded Florida to the United States in 1821, and pioneer settlements began in Key West. Bahamians—called "Conchs" because the sea snail was their dietary staple—and Cubans—from ninety nautical miles south—were the first to forge a life here, and a tough life it was. The hardy settlers endured hurricanes, mosquitos, sand fleas, extreme heat, isolation, no fresh water, no refrigeration, no electricity, no modern plumbing, and no medical aid! Culinary staples came in only occasionally by ship, so they survived on fish and seafood and grew fruits and vegetables in dooryard gardens.

Incorporated in 1828, Key West grew by leaps and bounds, becoming the largest and wealthiest city in the territory of Florida within ten years, even though it could only be reached by ship. And by 1900, Spanish was spoken as freely as English, as the two factions coexisted and intermarried. The word *Conch* came to be defined as any person descended from the original Bahamian or Cuban settlers of the Florida Keys. The Conch cuisine that began to evolve by the end of the century was a unique fusion of the English-Bahamian and Spanish-Cuban cultures—a combination of zesty Latin, spicy Caribbean, and traditional British influences coupled with the indigenous foodstuffs of the Keys.

Over the twentieth century, with Flagler's railroad and then the Overseas Highway linking the islands of the Keys with each other and the mainland, "strangers" and "washed-ashores" and eventually tourists from all over the globe "landed" in the Florida Keys and made it their home. This diverse group has contributed cultural and culinary influences to the melting pot, creating the Conch Fusion that has endured into the twenty-first century.

Cooking on the Rock

As you can see from this brief history, the people of the Florida Keys have come from far and wide. They tend to be individualistic, adventurous folk, attracted, perhaps, by the weather, the laid-back lifestyle, or just a desire for something different. And each has a story to tell.

You won't find much daylight between these Keysfolk and the talented restaurant chefs of the Florida Keys. Most happened here on a wing, or a whim, or a prayer—accidental tourists who found their culinary callings amidst our piscatorial wealth and startling sunsets. Many cooked at their mother's knee as a child or foraged in their grandmother's garden. Some trained at prestigious culinary institutes before joining our melting pot, but many started out at the bottom of the kitchen hierarchy, washing dishes and working their way up the line, restaurant by restaurant. All are in the kitchen because that is where their passions lie. They can't imagine themselves anywhere else.

These talented men and women chefs, the best of the best in the Florida Keys, bring unique culinary visions and concepts to their restaurants, fusing the flavors of their personal histories, travels, and cultures with our indigenous island ingredients. They paint a work of art on a plate, write a song of flavor notes, and compose a taste memory that will stay with you long after you leave our islands.

So, ladies and gentlemen, meet the chefs of the Florida Keys!

THE FLORIDA KEYS

Arranged by address and mile marker from Key Largo to Key West

The Fish House

102401 Overseas Highway, MM-102.4, Oceanside
Key Largo, FL 33037
(305) 451-4665
FISHHOUSE.COM
CJ Berwick and Doug Prew, Owners
Sam Quezada, Executive Chef

Burned out from their mainland jobs, Doug Prew and CJ Berwick landed in Key Largo in 1987 and bought a tiny little fish joint called the Fish House. "It was nothing," says Prew. "It had five employees and served about twenty meals a day, but we needed something operational because we knew absolutely nothing about running a restaurant."

Within a month, the couple found out just how steep their learning curve was going to be. The chef got mad and walked out, leaving Prew and Berwick scrambling. Prew called his brother, an amateur cook, and said, "I'm in trouble . . . I need a chef and you know how to cook." Brother came on board, their fish cutter donned an apron, and the drunken lunch cook carried on . . . drunk! In fact, says Berwick, "One day, drunk as usual, he accidentally put sherry in the Pan Sauté, and the customers loved it. So that is how the dish, our second most popular, is made to this day!"

Chef Sam Quezada came to the United States from his native Mexico when he was fourteen years old, living with an uncle in Homestead. He attended cooking classes at the tender age of nine and learned a lot about cooking at his grandmother's knee, but got his culinary training the old-fashioned way . . . from the bottom up. From his first jobs as dishwasher, prep cook, and then line cook at the Italian Fisherman restaurant, he honed his craft, joining the Fish House family as a line cook in 1989. "Everything is special here," says Sam, now head chef. "We work like a family. We enjoy coming to work. We have fun."

Evident to all, Prew and Berwick mastered their learning curve and the restaurant business because now, nearly thirty years later, the Fish House reigns as one of the most enduringly popular seafood roadhouse eateries in the Florida Keys. "Fresh, fresh, fresh fish and seafood" is the mantra here.

And it is still a family affair. Local fishermen daily bring their fresh catch directly to the back door, where they are filleted in-house. Prew's brother smokes fish for house specialties. Chef Sam's cousin Jose Ornelas bakes award-winning key lime pies and makes homemade ice creams. Jose's and Sam's kids bus tables. Berwick and Prew collect funky fishy decorations and twinkling lights, which adorn the walls and ceiling. "The Keys are a funky, kicked back, fun, crazy, upside-down place," says Prew. "It's different from that world up there, so we tried to keep that same feel." They did just that . . . and so much more!

Pasta with Shrimp & Cilantro-Lime Pesto

(SERVES 4)

For the pesto:

1¼ cups fresh cilantro leaves
¼ cup chopped scallions
3 tablespoons fresh lime juice
2 cloves garlic, pressed
1 tablespoon chopped, seeded jalapeño pepper
½ cup extra-virgin olive oil
Salt

For the pasta and shrimp:

Salt
1 pound linguine
1 tablespoon extra-virgin olive oil
1 pound medium shrimp, peeled and deveined
3 tablespoons tequila
Freshly ground black pepper
¼ cup crumbled Cotija cheese or feta cheese
¼ cup chopped fresh cilantro

To make the pesto: Up to 1 day ahead: Place cilantro leaves, scallions, lime juice, garlic, and jalapeños in a food processor and pulse until mixture is a coarse puree. With machine running, gradually add olive oil. Season with salt to taste. Transfer to a covered container and refrigerate until needed.

To prepare the pasta and shrimp: Cook linguine in a large pot of salted boiling water until al dente (tender but firm to the bite), stirring occasionally. Drain and set aside.

Meanwhile, warm pesto in a medium saucepan over low heat. Place olive oil in a large heavy skillet over medium-high heat. Add shrimp and sauté until almost opaque in center, about 3 minutes, stirring frequently. Remove skillet from heat and add tequila. Return skillet to heat and stir until sauce thickens slightly, about 30 seconds. Add pesto and stir until shrimp are coated with sauce.

Remove skillet from heat. Add pasta to skillet and toss with shrimp and pesto sauce. Season with salt and pepper to taste. Divide shrimp and pasta evenly among 4 plates. Sprinkle each portion with 1 tablespoon cheese and 1 tablespoon chopped cilantro.

SHRIMP BUNDLES WITH BASIL & PROSCIUTTO

(SERVES 2 AS AN APPETIZER)

2 tablespoons vegetable oil

1 teaspoon lemon juice

1 tablespoon honey

1 tablespoon fresh minced garlic

10 large shrimp, peeled and deveined

5 basil leaves, each snipped in half

10 slices prosciutto

Vegetable cooking spray

Preheat oven to 450°F. Mix oil, lemon juice, honey, and garlic in a medium-size bowl. Add shrimp and toss with marinade. Marinate shrimp for 5 minutes. Remove shrimp with a slotted spoon and place on a medium plate. Reserve marinade.

Place 1 shrimp and ½ basil leaf atop 1 prosciutto slice. Fold in sides and roll to wrap into a bundle. Secure with a toothpick. Repeat process with remaining shrimp, basil leaves, and prosciutto slices.

Place shrimp bundles in a lightly oiled baking dish. Pour reserved marinade over bundles. Bake for 5 minutes. Remove toothpicks and place 5 bundles on each of 2 plates.

The Fish House Encore

102341 Overseas Highway, MM-102.3, Oceanside
Key Largo, FL 33037
(305) 451-0650
FISHHOUSE.COM
CJ Berwick and Doug Prew, Owners
Peter Tseleksis, Executive Chef

"We bought the property next door to the Fish House," say Doug Prew and CJ Berwick, "mainly to have more parking. But then we wondered, 'What should we do with the building?'" Prew became intrigued by the piano bar concept he had seen on a Jamaican vacation. "So, in 2002, we decided to open a music-themed upscale restaurant with a more relaxed dining environment than the Fish House."

Encore was born. A sleek piano bar lounge, crystal- and linen-topped tables in a formal dining room, and a tropical patio set the stage for an extensive menu with worldwide influences, including a raw bar and full sushi menu. "Actually, we eventually had to make it a little less elegant," says Berwick. "People would peek in and say it was too fancy for them and then leave. So we added some fish nets and 'Keysed' it up a bit."

Greek-born Peter Tseleksis joined Encore when it first opened, as a line cook. "In the first four months, four chefs came and went," says Tseleksis. "I was the last man standing," which proved a serendipitous event for him. Now executive chef, Tseleksis traversed continents before ending up in the Florida Keys. Emigrating to Canada in 1973 at the age of seventeen, Tseleksis faced a language barrier that propelled him into a restaurant kitchen as a dishwasher. After stints as a soda fountain jerk and a night short-order cook, he apprenticed at a string of Toronto restaurants, finally earning "the keys to the kitchen" and becoming a bona fide chef.

In 1992 the Greek owner of Perry's restaurant in Key West sponsored Tseleksis to come to America. He worked at Perry's, first in Key West and then in Key Largo, until he joined Encore. Whereas diners

can get some of the same fresh seafood selections as are offered at the Fish House, Tseleksis takes pleasure in creating nightly specials of premium meats as well as the fish and pasta "presentations of the week." His Greek heritage definitely influences his cuisine, he says. Dill, garlic, oregano, and basil are among his favorite seasonings, but he doesn't use many herbs and spices together. "I think less is more," Tseleksis says. "I don't like to confuse the palate."

FISH FLAGLER

(SERVES 4)

1 (12-ounce) can roasted red peppers, drained and julienned

1 (24-ounce) can artichoke hearts, drained and quartered

1 pound fresh asparagus, trimmed and sliced thin on the diagonal

12 scallions, sliced on the diagonal

½ cup extra-virgin olive oil

¼ cup white wine

3 ounces fresh lime juice

1 tablespoon fresh chopped garlic

Salt and freshly ground black pepper

4 (8-ounce) fish fillets, cut thick

Eight hours ahead: Place peppers, artichoke hearts, asparagus, scallions, olive oil, white wine, lime juice, and garlic in a large covered container. Season with salt and pepper to taste. Refrigerate for 8 hours.

Preheat gas grill to hot and oven to 350°F. Season fish fillets with salt and pepper to taste. Grill fillets to medium-rare, about 3–6 minutes, depending upon the thickness of the fillets. Remove fillets from grill and place on a greased baking sheet. Using a slotted spoon, top each fillet with one-quarter of the mixed vegetables. Pour about ½ cup of the vegetable marinade atop vegetable-topped fillets. Bake for 10 minutes. Serve immediately with rice or potatoes.

Encore Pumpkin Bisque with Crabmeat

(SERVES 6–8)

2 tablespoons butter

1 teaspoon minced garlic

1 small sweet onion, like Vidalia, chopped

2 stalks celery, chopped

½ teaspoon freshly ground nutmeg

½ teaspoon ground cinnamon

1 tablespoon brown sugar

1 (28-ounce) can pure pumpkin

1 cup chicken stock

2 cups heavy cream

½ cup sherry

Salt and freshly ground black pepper

6 ounces lump crabmeat

Melt butter in a large saucepan over medium-high heat. Add garlic, onions, and celery and sauté for 2 minutes, stirring frequently. Add nutmeg, cinnamon, and brown sugar and stir to mix well. Stir in pumpkin and chicken stock. Reduce heat to medium and cook for 15 minutes, stirring occasionally.

Stir in cream and bring mixture to a boil. Reduce heat to low and cook for 15 minutes. Stir in sherry and cook for 5 minutes more. Season with salt and pepper to taste. Stir in crabmeat, taking care not to break the pieces up too much. Serve immediately.

Key Largo Conch House

100211 Overseas Highway, MM-100.2, Oceanside
Key Largo, FL 33037
(305) 453-4844
KEYLARGOCONCHHOUSE.COM
Laura and Ted Dreaver, Owners

For twenty-five years, diving aficionados Ted and Laura Dreaver vacationed in the Florida Keys. "When you get here, you never want to leave," states Ted. "We asked ourselves, 'What could we do here that we could just stay?'" Ted decided a restaurant might be a good choice.

"I've heard a lot of dreams in the thirty-five years we've been together, so I never thought he'd do it," says Laura. "In 2004, when he said he'd found a restaurant to buy—Frank Keys Cafe in Key Largo—I thought, 'Oh no!'" The Dreavers had no experience in the restaurant business, but says Ted, "I had been a project manager dealing with major corporations. I thought, 'How hard can this be? We'll figure it out.'"

Calling the restaurant Key Largo Coffee House, they decided to start small, with coffees and smoothies, breakfasts, and light lunch items. The Dreavers experimented at home, developing menu items like Laura's Tuna Apple Wrap, which became so popular that it's still on the menu. "It was actually very difficult," Ted says. "We didn't make any money for the first two years." Adds Laura, "We were like, 'Oh my God, what were we thinking?' Then suddenly everything took off."

The Dreavers expanded to offer dinner in addition to breakfast and lunch, and since the restaurant is housed in a charming Conch-style house nestled in a tropical hammock, they changed the name to Key Largo Conch House. Seafood is Conch House's specialty, coming fresh off the boats, a stone's throw away, from Key Largo Fisheries. Their signature dish? Lobster Benedict. "We put a whole lobster tail right on top of the benedict," says Laura.

What started as the snowbirds' dream has morphed into a Keys reality for the Midwestern couple, who have been featured on the Food Network and the Travel Channel. The Dreavers give full credit to their talented staff, both front and back of the house. "We are a family," they say.

Lobster Bisque

(SERVES 8)

3 spiny (Florida) lobster tails
½ cup tomato paste
¾ cup chopped onions
¾ cup chopped celery
¾ cup chopped carrots
2 tablespoons olive oil
1½ teaspoons salt
1 tablespoon freshly ground black pepper
2 tablespoons flour
2 tablespoons water
3 cups heavy cream

Fill a large pot three-quarters full with water. Place over high heat and bring to a boil. When water boils, add lobster tails. Reduce heat to medium-high and simmer, uncovered, for 20 minutes, until lobsters have turned red.

Remove lobster tails and reserve 5 cups of stock. (Discard rest of stock; wash and dry pot.) Remove all meat from tails. Discard shells. Finely chop lobster meat. (You should have at least ¾ cup lobster meat.) Place lobster meat in pot. Add reserved lobster stock and tomato paste and simmer on medium heat for 30 minutes, stirring occasionally.

Meanwhile, place onions, celery, and carrots in a food processor and process until finely minced. Place oil in a large sauté pan over medium heat. Add vegetable mixture and sauté for 5 minutes, stirring frequently. Season with salt and pepper. Mix flour and 2 tablespoons water in a small bowl. Add to simmering vegetable mixture. Cook for 10 minutes, stirring occasionally. Add vegetable mixture to lobster pot.

Slowly whisk in cream. Reduce heat to low and simmer for 20 minutes, until thickened. Serve immediately.

Snook's Bayside

99470 Overseas Highway, MM-99.4, Bayside
Key Largo, FL 33037
(305) 453-5004
SNOOKS.COM
Roni Hammer and Jennifer Hammer, Owners
Gasline Marcelin, Executive Chef

Literally "up from the ashes" after being totally destroyed by a devastating fire in 2010, the reincarnation of Snook's Bayside is a little like sophisticated South Beach meets West Indian island casual. The open-air restaurant, which sits aside the sweeping waters of Florida Bay under a grand tiki, is *the* place to go for an Upper Keys sunset celebration.

"Every day we have a Sunset Horn Celebration," says owner Roni Hammer. "We have a rope attached to an old boat horn. We randomly select someone in the restaurant, give them our signature rum drink served in a hollowed-out coconut, and have them pull the rope to blow the horn, ushering in the sunset," she describes. "Then the live music begins." As darkness closes in, flickering tiki torches dramatically transform the entire place into a romantic island oasis.

Hammer wholeheartedly endorses her executive chef, Haitian-born Gasline Marcelin, who joined her kitchen in 1997 and worked up the line over the years, honing his craft. "He's a wonderful human being," she says of Gasline. "He brings that to everything he does in this restaurant . . . his respect for the staff, for the kitchen, for me, for our

guests." Marcelin modestly credits Snook's former executive chef for his excellent tutelage. "Chef Tony was a very, very unselfish person," says Marcelin. "He taught me everything he knew. Because of him, I am what I am today."

Marcelin describes his cuisine as parts American, Spanish, Italian, and his native Creole. Creating more than 200 meals a night from the small, new, open-face kitchen proved to be a challenge at first. "I was used to the other kitchen, which was very big," he says. "But," he goes on, "I always cook with love and passion. I believe if you always start to cook with a positive mind-set, you'll enjoy what you're cooking."

Marcelin lives his own philosophy. "I love to cook!" he proclaims. Love is his favorite ingredient, he unabashedly states. "I'm always in a good mood," he says. "Always, no matter what. The only way to make things perfect is to put everybody in a good mood!"

PISTACHIO-ENCRUSTED YELLOWTAIL SNAPPER WITH SWEET CHILI SAUCE

(SERVES 1)

For the snapper:

¼ cup ground pistachio nuts
1 (7-ounce) yellowtail snapper fillet
2 tablespoons unsalted butter

For the sweet chili sauce:

3 tablespoons unsalted butter, divided
1 teaspoon minced shallots
3 ounces heavy cream
Salt and freshly ground black pepper
1 teaspoon (bottled) Asian sweet chili sauce

¼ cup cubed (no larger than ½ inch) fresh mango

To prepare the yellowtail snapper: Place ground pistachios on a large plate. Dredge both sides of snapper fillet in nuts. Melt 2 tablespoons butter in a large sauté pan over medium heat. Place snapper fillet in sauté pan and cook for 5 minutes. Turn fillet and cook for 2–5 minutes more, until fish is golden brown and flakes when tested with a fork.

To make the sweet chili sauce: Meanwhile, place a medium sauté pan over medium heat for 2–3 minutes. Add 2 tablespoons butter and shallots and sauté until shallots are softened. Add cream and reduce until it thickens somewhat. Stir in 1 tablespoon butter and season with salt and pepper to taste. Simmer for 5 minutes. Stir in Asian sweet chili sauce.

To plate and serve: Place yellowtail snapper fillet in the center of a dinner plate. Top with mango cubes. Pour sweet chili sauce over the mango-topped snapper and serve immediately.

HAZELNUT CHICKEN

(SERVES 1)

For the chicken:

¼ cup crushed hazelnut flour
1 (7-ounce) boneless, skinless chicken breast
2 tablespoons butter

For the hazelnut sauce:

1 tablespoon butter
1 teaspoon chopped shallots
1 teaspoon snipped fresh thyme
2 ounces hazelnut liqueur
2 ounces fresh orange juice
4 ounces heavy cream
Salt and freshly ground black pepper
¼ cup canned mandarin oranges

Sprig of parsley

To prepare the chicken: Place flour on a large plate. Dredge both sides of chicken in flour. Melt the 2 tablespoons butter in a large sauté pan over medium-high heat. Place chicken breast in sauté pan and cook for 5 minutes. Turn chicken breast and cook for 5 minutes more, until just cooked through.

To make the hazelnut sauce: Meanwhile, place a medium saucepan over medium heat for 2–3 minutes. Add butter, shallots, thyme, liqueur, orange juice, cream, and salt and pepper to taste. Simmer for 5 minutes. Stir in mandarin oranges.

To plate and serve: Place chicken breast in the center of a dinner plate. Top chicken with hazelnut sauce and garnish with a sprig of parsley. Serve immediately.

Key Largo Fisheries

1313 Ocean Bay Drive, MM-99.4, Oceanside
Key Largo, FL 33037
(305) 451-3784
KEYLARGOFISHERIES.COM
Dottie Hill, Tom Hill, and Rick Hill, Owners

Fish has been in the DNA of the Hill family for generations, starting with Tom Hill's lobster-fisherman grandfather back in the early 1940s. Tom's father, Jack, himself a lobsterman, took over the family boat in 1965 and moved the family to Key Largo from Miami. Tom was fifteen years old and, with his brother Rick, caught ballyhoo and sold them as bait to tackle stores from the back of a pickup truck.

In 1972, needing a brick-and-mortar structure from which to sell Jack's lobsters and the boys' bait, the family "dug holes and poured concrete," creating the building that today is Key Largo Fisheries. "Other fishermen asked if we'd buy their fish and sell them at our place," recalls Hill. "Pretty soon we were too busy to fish."

Fast-forwarding to 2014 finds Key Largo Fisheries selling about 400,000 pounds of Florida lobster a year, mostly exported to China with a high price tag, to satisfy their constant demand. And the Just Rite Bait product line processes 20,000 cases of ballyhoo a year. With a fleet of thirty-five to forty boats bringing in fresh catch every day, the fishery also supplies restaurants from Key West to Fort Lauderdale daily and air expresses fish overnight to eateries across the United States every week. "One Ohio restaurant told me that our fish has made them the number one seafood restaurant in Toledo," says Hill.

Key Largo Fisheries started smoking fish back in the 1980s. Hill's mother, Dottie, "started playing around with making a smoked fish dip to sell in our retail market," says Hill. "It was trial and error until she came up with something everyone loved." Today the fishery's mixer can turn out 150 pounds of the perfected recipe at a time.

In 2010 Key Largo Fisheries opened an eatery of their own in the backyard of the business, aptly named the Backyard Cafe. With nothing more than an order window and a bunch of picnic tables along the dock, the cafe

quickly caught on and its menu grew and grew. Besides creating the signature sandwich, the Lobster BLT, Hill, his daughter Carrie Pino, and the talented cooks behind the scenes function as something of a test kitchen as well, developing the seafood salads, dips, and sauces sold in the cafe and retail fish market.

Hill sees technology and government regulations as the biggest challenges for fishermen to make a living these days. But it is still a far cry from the day his grandfather traded 300 pounds of lobster for a Thanksgiving turkey.

DOTTIE'S KEY LARGO SMOKED FISH DIP

(SERVES 4–6 AS AN APPETIZER)

1 pound smoked fish
6 tablespoons salad cubes*
1¼ cups mayonnaise
1 cup sour cream
8 ounces cream cheese, softened
2 tablespoons Worcestershire sauce
½ teaspoon cayenne pepper
Juice of ½ lemon
½ cup chopped green bell peppers
½ cup chopped celery
¼ cup chopped red or white (or mixture) onions
Freshly ground black pepper, optional
Tabasco sauce, optional
Crackers

Place smoked fish in a food processor and pulse until ground finely (or to your liking). Transfer fish to a large covered container. Add salad cubes, mayonnaise, sour cream, cream cheese, Worcestershire sauce, cayenne pepper, and lemon juice. Stir to mix well.

Add bell peppers, celery, and onions and stir to mix well. Add black pepper and/or Tabasco to taste. Cover container and refrigerate until needed. Serve with crackers.

*Salad cubes are a lot like relish but sweeter. You can find them in the same grocery aisle as the relish and pickles.

M.E.A.T.

88005 Overseas Highway, MM-88, Oceanside
Islamorada, FL 33036
(305) 852-3833
MEATEATERY.COM
George Adam Patti, Chef and Owner
Tom Smith, Sommelier and Owner

When George Patti and Tom Smith opened M.E.A.T. (Meat Eatery and Taproom) in Islamorada in 2012, people told them, "You're crazy. We're in the middle of a fishing village." "Exactly!" said Patti. Adds Smith, "People laughed at us. 'Those guys are idiots,' they said. 'What are they trying to do? And they're going to call it M.E.A.T.?'"

Patti and Smith have the last laugh now. Their concept for M.E.A.T.—a carnivorous oasis surrounded by the sea—rapidly caught on. "Everything is smoked, ground, and cured in-house," says Patti. "We wanted to do good sandwiches, homemade sausages, house-cured bacon, and house-ground beef burgers." And while the Inside-Out Juicy Lucy Burger may very well be the twenty-first-century "Cheeseburger in Paradise," Patti says, "It was really about the sausages for me."

Patti grew up in New Rochelle, New York, where his father owned a deli. "I was prepping for him by age twelve," he recalls. "We used to make our own brisket, pastrami, Italian sausage, and bratwurst." At M.E.A.T. Patti cures his bacon for three weeks in a mixture of salt, sugar, rosemary, black pepper, onion powder, garlic powder, and maple syrup. "It sells like crazy," he says. And ketchup, mustard, and Worcestershire sauce are made in-house as well.

The two business partners met in Islamorada, when Smith, a certified sommelier since 1997, was general manager of Marker 88 and Patti, who holds both culinary and business degrees, was food and beverage chief at Holiday Isle. They began teaching cooking classes with wine pairings that became wildly popular. "George is very talented with food," says Smith. "He has a huge passion for it. I've studied wines. I have a huge passion for wine and craft beers." Opening a restaurant together seemed like a natural.

Patti and Smith opened their latest joint endeavor, S.A.L.T—Southern Asian Latin Tastes—in Islamorada in March 2014. They see the concept as a fusion of fun global flavors, beautifully presented on composed plates. "Everything has a meaning," says Patti. "You use all your taste buds. We want your palate to wake up," he says. "I work the front of the house and select wines that work with George's food," says Smith. Patti adds, "The ingredients work together and complement each other." Much like George Patti and Tom Smith, the food and wine gurus, themselves.

M.E.A.T.'s Signature Ketchup

(MAKES 22 OUNCES)

12 pounds ripe tomatoes, quartered

1½ teaspoons kosher salt

6 whole Vidalia onions, cut into chunks

3 whole garlic cloves

1 tablespoon ground cardamom

1 (7-ounce) can chipotle chilies in adobo sauce

4 (12-ounce) jars mango chutney

3 teaspoons ground allspice

2 tablespoons chopped fresh gingerroot

4 small bay leaves

3 pints (48 ounces) white vinegar

6½ cups tomato paste

2 tablespoons sugar

Preheat oven to 400°F. Place tomatoes in a large ovenproof saucepan in layers. Sprinkle each layer with a little salt. Cover and refrigerate overnight.

Add onions, garlic, cardamom, chipotles and adobo sauce, chutney, allspice, gingerroot, and bay leaves. Stir to mix well. Place saucepan over medium-low heat and bring to a simmer. Cover saucepan, transfer it to oven, and braise mixture for 1 hour or until thick.

Return saucepan to stove over low heat. Add vinegar, tomato paste, and sugar and simmer for 20 minutes, stirring frequently, or until mixture has a thickened syrupy consistency. Remove bay leaves. Transfer to a blender and puree in batches until very smooth.

Pour ketchup into glass bottles, covered containers, or mason jars and refrigerate for up to 2 months. Ketchup can be frozen.

Inside-Out Juicy Lucy Burger

(SERVES 1)

6 ounces (80/20) ground beef
1 (1-ounce) slice cheddar cheese
2 ounces pimento cheese spread
Favorite burger spice blend
1 challah bun
1 tablespoon melted butter
M.E.A.T.'s Signature Ketchup
1 leaf iceberg lettuce
1 slice tomato

Make two 3-ounce ground beef patties. Place cheddar cheese slice atop one patty. Spread pimento cheese atop the other patty. Put the two patties together so that all the cheese is in the middle. Press the patties together and crimp the edges so that all the cheese is sealed in the middle of the burger. Season with spice blend to taste.

Heat a gas or charcoal grill or a flattop griddle. Cook the burger to medium-rare, about 2 minutes on each side. Toast bun lightly and brush cut sides with melted butter. Serve burger on bun with M.E.A.T.'s Signature Ketchup, lettuce, and tomato.

19200 SW 344th Street
Homestead, FL 33034
(305) 246-1592
ROBERTISHERE.COM
Robert Moehling, Owner

"My dad was dead broke," recalls Robert Moehling, describing how his renowned Homestead fruit and vegetable stand was born one November day in 1959. "He had harvested 400 bushels of cucumbers," he says of his farmer father, "and the produce broker wouldn't take them. So on Saturday, my dad put a piece of plywood on top of a couple of field crates on the corner of our property, dumped a pile of cucumbers on it, and told me to sell them."

"I was six years old," says Moehling, "and I sat there all day. Nobody stopped." The next day Moehling was back on the corner again, but this time his father put big signs—made from hurricane shutters—on either side of the table, that said in big red letters, "Robert Is Here." "I sold out by noon and walked home," he says.

The signs, the stand, and Robert sat on that corner the following weekend, and every weekend after that. He added zucchinis, yellow squash, and other things the family grew. "Other farmers saw this fat, little kid sittin' there, and they brought tomatoes and corn and asked me to sell them," he recalls. "For the first few weekends, nothing cost me a penny."

Moehling's mother decided they should sell vegetables every day, so she put a coffee can on the vegetable table and people paid for their produce on the honor system. "The school bus driver would drop me off at the corner," Moehling says, "and I'd collect the money from the can and take care of customers until it got dark and it was time to go home for dinner." The business grew and the plywood stand was replaced by a small building, right next to the road. Today's Robert Is Here sits on that very spot. And its roof, painted in giant letters, proclaims "Robert Is Here."

Moehling bought his first ten acres of farmland when he was fourteen years old. Now he has sixty. "I grow most of the weird stuff," he says, "papayas, avocados, mangoes, mamey sapotes, lichees, guanabanas (sour sops), and monstera deliciosa." He remembers, "I used to aggravate John Tower, who had a hundred acres of grove next to our farm. As a little kid, I used to ride with his workers, and he taught me how to graft avocado and mango trees. He had all the weird mameys and sugar apples and I'd talk him into selling them to me, and I would sell them here," he says. "It was stuff no one ever saw before," he goes on, "and it made us special. It still makes us special."

Also unique at Robert Is Here is the checkout process. Workers write item prices on a paper bag, then compute the sum by hand and head. "That's my fault," says Moehling. "I'm dyslexic and can't bring the numbers from the item to the cash register. But I can add them in up-and-down columns." No one can work at Robert Is Here unless they are able to add accurately in their head, without a cash register. Applicants must successfully pass multiple addition tests before he will even allow them to fill out an application form.

Robert Is Here evolved over the years to become a tourist destination as well as being perhaps the coolest fruit stand in existence. "I've been a farm boy all my life," says Moehling. "Farm boys have their animals," he says, explaining the emus, goats, donkeys, and geese out back. Live music is played on weekends and holidays, adding to the festive atmosphere.

The walls are lined with unusual sauces, preserves, and jellies, many from recipes his mother made long ago. And the shakes . . . oh, the shakes! "We started making fruit shakes over thirty years ago," Moehling says, "because my mom couldn't use up all the extra fruit making jam. We don't use sugar in our shakes, just fruit and ice cream."

Moehling personally thinks guanabana is the most magnificent flavor of any fruit grown. "It's almost like a religious experience," he says. "It makes you feel so good after you eat it." But he says canistel (eggfruit) probably makes the very best shake. Canistel is in the sapote family. You use the whole fruit and just have to remove a couple of seeds and the stem. "When it is ripe, it takes the texture of room-temperature butter," Moehling says. "It's like the inside of a cream-filled doughnut."

Robert Is Here is very much a family affair, as Moehling's wife, four children, and their spouses all are involved in the business. "When you enter my place, the aura is way different than any other fruit and vegetable market," states Moehling. "This is something that can't happen again," he says, "because you can't have a six-year-old sitting on the side of the road anymore, anywhere. We don't want it to end."

And in case you were wondering, Robert IS here, every day of the week!

Canistel Strawberry Shake

(SERVES 1)

1 cup canistel, seeds and stem removed
1½ cups sliced strawberries
12 ounces vanilla ice cream

Place ingredients in a blender and blend until smooth. Serve in a tall milkshake glass.

Ziggie & Mad Dog's

83000 Overseas Highway, MM-83, Bayside
Islamorada, FL 33036
(305) 664-3391
ZIGGIEANDMADDOGS.COM
Benjamin Coole, Executive Chef

"We're all pirates here," says executive chef Ben Coole, when speaking about his top-notch culinary team at Ziggie & Mad Dog's. Emblematic scarf tied around his head, two-foot ponytail braid snaking down his back, the rugged, imposing, English-born chef credits his staff as the brilliance behind the restaurant's cuisine. "A restaurant is nothing without its crew—just a building with food," he maintains.

But both the building and the food at Ziggie & Mad Dog's have been legendary for decades. Originally an outbuilding on a pineapple plantation, the structure was turned into a fine-dining restaurant, Ziggie's Conch, in 1962 by Sigmund "Ziggie" Stocki. No-frills, great food, and a colorful clientele established Ziggie's as the go-to place in Islamorada until the untimely death in 1992 of Ziggie's son Alan, who had been running the restaurant since Ziggie's passing in 1977.

Thirteen years later, former Miami Dolphins tight end Jim "Mad Dog" Mandich, South Florida sportscaster Randy Kassewitz, and restaurateur John Atkinson restored Ziggie's to its former glory and burnished its traditions with a shiny new image. "Mad Dog wanted Fred Flintstone–cut steaks, salads, and sides," says Coole, "athlete-size portions big enough to share." He describes the cuisine concept at Ziggie & Mad Dog's as "classic American with a twist—really good, fresh, simple cooking" accompanied by house-made butters, rubs, and complex sauces.

Trained in classical French style at University of West London, Coole traveled

the world as a young chef, picking up ideas from other chefs he worked with in such far-flung countries as Israel, South Africa, and Honduras. Enamored with the Florida Keys since a holiday visit in his youth, he returned to Key West, met a girl, fell in love, got married, and stayed.

Now, fifteen years later, Coole presides over one of the most storied kitchens in the Florida Keys. Creating new dishes is a collaborative effort, he says. "If we have time, we'll have a mess-around day and we'll just play with stuff in the kitchen." Advises the pirate chef, "To get your own style, you have to break a few rules. Cooking should be fun. Don't give up."

Smothered Tenderloin Medallions

(SERVES 1)

For the au poivre sauce:

2 teaspoons olive oil
2 cloves garlic, finely chopped
1 cup heavy cream, divided
1 cup beef stock
4 tablespoons butter
2 ounces brandy
1 tablespoon coarse-ground black pepper

For the onions:

1 large red onion, peeled
1 leek
1 tablespoon olive oil
2 teaspoons brown sugar
Salt and freshly ground black pepper
2 tablespoons butter
2 ounces brandy

For the mashed potatoes:

8 ounces red creamer potatoes, rinsed and quartered
Salt
6 tablespoons butter
3 ounces heavy cream
Freshly ground black pepper
Pinch of nutmeg

For the medallions:

9-ounce beef tenderloin, cut into 3 equal medallions
Salt and freshly ground black pepper

2 ounces Stilton cheese, crumbled

To make the au poivre sauce: Place olive oil in a 10-inch sauté pan over medium heat. Add garlic and sauté for 1 minute, until garlic is soft but not browned. Add cream, beef stock, butter, brandy, and pepper. Cook sauce, stirring constantly with a wire whisk, until sauce is thick and rich. (Watch carefully so that sauce does not boil over.) Remove sauce from heat and set aside until needed. Before serving, warm sauce over low heat. (If sauce splits because of excessive reheating, add a splash of heavy cream.)

To prepare the onions: Cut onion in half and slice each half into half-moon pieces. Cut top and bottom off leek and remove tough outer layers. Cut leek in half lengthwise. Wash leek thoroughly, making sure to rinse between layers, and pat dry with paper towels. Cut leek into half-moon slices. Place olive oil in a large sauté pan over high heat until almost smoking. Carefully add onions and leeks. Sprinkle with brown sugar and add a pinch of salt and pepper.

Sauté onions and leeks, stirring constantly, for 2 ½ minutes. Reduce heat to medium and sauté for another 2½ minutes, stirring constantly. Add butter and brandy. Reduce heat to low and simmer mixture until onions are light brown, soft, and caramelized. Remove from heat and set aside.

To make the mashed potatoes: Place potatoes in a large saucepan over medium heat with water to cover. Add a pinch of salt and boil until potatoes are cooked through. Drain potatoes and return them to the saucepan. Add butter, cream, salt and pepper to taste, and a pinch of nutmeg. Mash potatoes to desired consistency.

To prepare the tenderloin medallions: Preheat gas or charcoal grill until very hot. Season medallions with salt and pepper to taste. Grill medallions to medium-rare. Be careful not to overcook the meat.

To assemble: Preheat oven broiler. Place mashed potatoes in the center of a dinner plate, mounding them in a pyramid shape that peaks in the middle. Arrange medallions evenly around the mashed potatoes, leaning them on the potatoes so that they stretch about halfway up. Spoon the onion/leek mixture over the peak of the mashed potatoes, semi-covering the top of the medallions. Drizzle a little onion/leek pan juice on top. Sprinkle crumbled Stilton atop onions and spoon au poivre sauce over onions and medallions. Place under broiler briefly, just until cheese begins to melt and serve immediately.

White Truffle Lobster Mac & Cheese

(SERVES 2 AS AN APPETIZER OR A SIDE)

1 (6–8 ounce) Florida lobster tail

2 teaspoons olive oil

2 cloves garlic, finely chopped

4 tablespoons butter

1 pint (16 ounces) heavy cream, divided

8 ounces grated white cheddar cheese, divided

4 ounces grated Parmesan cheese, divided

6–8 fresh basil leaves, snipped into chiffonade

6–8 cherry tomatoes, quartered

1 roasted red bell pepper, cut into bite-size pieces
(see sidebar)

4 ounces brandy

3–4 cups cooked pasta shells

1 teaspoon truffle oil

2 tablespoons chopped fresh parsley

2 lemon wedges

To prepare the lobster: Preheat oven to 350°F. Place lobster on a cutting board and insert knife at the base of the top side of the tail where the meat ends, leaving the tail fan intact. Cut through the top shell and meat only, leaving the underside intact, and remove lobster meat. Rinse lobster meat and dry it with paper towels to remove any shell particles and fecal line. Dice lobster meat into bite-size pieces and set aside. Open up the shell and place in hot oven for a couple of minutes, until the shell turns orangey red. Remove shell from oven and set aside.

To make the lobster mac and cheese: Place olive oil in a large sauté pan over medium heat. Add garlic and sauté until soft but not browned. Add butter, 1 cup heavy cream, 6 ounces grated cheddar, and half the Parmesan cheese. Stir with a small whisk until cheese begins to melt into the cream. Reduce heat to medium-low. Add basil, cherry tomatoes, roasted red peppers, and reserved lobster meat.

Continue simmering the mixture, stirring frequently, until sauce thickens and lobster is cooked through. Add remaining heavy cream, brandy, pasta shells, and truffle oil. Stir mixture and continue cooking a minute or two, until sauce is hot, thick, rich, and bubbly.

To serve: Preheat oven broiler. Place lobster tail shell on an ovenproof serving plate. Pour lobster mac and cheese into the shell, allowing it to spill over sides of shell onto the serving plate. Top with remaining grated cheddar and Parmesan cheeses. Place under broiler briefly, just until cheeses melt. Sprinkle with chopped parsley and garnish with lemon wedges.

ATLANTIC'S EDGE

81801 OVERSEAS HIGHWAY, MM-81.8, OCEANSIDE
ISLAMORADA, FL 33036
(800) 327-2888
CHEECA.COM/DINING/ATLANTICSEDGE
RICHARD SMITH, EXECUTIVE CHEF

Upscale elegance and cuisine coupled with an island ambience and one of the most panoramically beautiful oceanfront settings in the Keys personify Atlantic's Edge at Islamorada's Cheeca Lodge & Spa. "I fell in love with it immediately," states Jamaican-born executive chef Richard Smith. "It reminds me of the Caribbean islands."

Smith came to Florida in 1998 to study business administration at Tallahassee

Community College and FSU. "I really didn't like it," he says. "Cooking was my first love. I used to watch my parents in the kitchen making the most amazing food," he recalls of his childhood. "My mother made fantastic Jamaican food; my dad did international things, like pastas."

Every day after his business classes, Smith watched the Emeril Lagasse show on the Food Network, fascinated. His idol, Lagasse, said he had studied culinary arts at Johnson & Wales, so Smith decided to transfer to the school's Miami campus, where he earned a dual degree in culinary arts and food service management, all the while working the line full-time at such restaurants as the Ritz Carlton South Beach.

"I remember being on the fence while at the Ritz, not sure if I wanted to do front of the house or be in the kitchen," he says. "The chef de cuisine there was a wonderful culinarian. He was doing food I'd never seen before. He inspired and motivated me to be a good chef."

Smith pulls from his Jamaican roots to add a Caribbean flair to his international cuisine at Atlantic's Edge, which he joined as executive chef in 2012. "We have a formal yet laid-back atmosphere. We try not to do any foo-foo food," he says with a laugh. "I'm still back there cooking," he adds. "We use a lot of fresh seasonal produce from the farms up in Homestead as a starting point for creating new dishes. It is a collaborative effort."

When asked what he considers most special about Atlantic's Edge, he credits his staff—both front and back of the house—many of whom are from the islands. "And you cannot beat this view," he adds.

Hogfish à la Plancha

(SERVES 2)

For the salt cod croquettes:

½ pound skinless, boneless salt cod

1 cup milk

2 thyme sprigs

1 bay leaf

2 cloves garlic, smashed

1 pound Yukon Gold potatoes, peeled and
   cut into 1-inch chunks

1 tablespoon extra-virgin olive oil

1 large shallot, diced

3 cloves garlic, minced

3 tablespoons chopped cilantro

1 large egg yolk

3 large whole eggs

1 cup all-purpose flour

1 cup fine bread crumbs

Vegetable oil for frying

For the carambola and clementine beurre blanc:

3 carambolas (star fruit)

Juice of 3 clementines

1 (750 ml) bottle white wine

1 cup sugar

1 vanilla bean, halved and seeded

1 cup butter, cut into small cubes

1 lime

Salt

For the fish:

2 (6-ounce) hogfish fillets, skin on, scaled, and cleaned

Salt and freshly ground black pepper

2 tablespoons extra-virgin olive oil

For the wilted brassica:

1 tablespoon extra-virgin olive oil

2 cups brassica (baby mustard greens), cleaned

Salt and freshly ground black pepper

To make the salt cod croquettes: Place salt cod
in a medium bowl. Cover cod with cold water and
refrigerate for 24 hours or up to 2 days. Change
the water at least 3 times.

Drain salt cod and transfer it to a large saucepan.
Add milk, thyme, bay leaf, and smashed garlic.
Add water to the pan to cover the fish by 2
inches. Simmer over low heat for 20 minutes, until
the fish flakes with a fork. Transfer fish to a plate
and allow it to cool. Flake fish and set aside.

Place potatoes in a medium saucepan with water
to cover and simmer over medium heat until tender, about 10 minutes. Transfer potatoes to a large
bowl along with 2 tablespoons of the cooking liquid. Mash potatoes to a coarse puree. Set aside.

Place olive oil in a small sauté pan over medium-
high heat. Add shallots and minced garlic and
cook until soft, stirring occasionally, about 5
minutes. Transfer mixture to bowl of potatoes.
Add flaked salt cod, cilantro, and egg yolk and
stir until well mixed. Cover bowl and refrigerate
mixture at least 30 minutes, until well chilled.

Whisk eggs and 1 teaspoon water in a small bowl.
Place flour and bread crumbs in separate small
bowls. Line a baking sheet with wax paper. Form
the salt cod mixture into 1-inch balls. Dredge
balls in flour, then dip them in the beaten eggs,
then dredge them in bread crumbs until well
coated. Arrange the croquettes on the prepared
baking sheet and refrigerate until chilled, about 15
minutes, or until needed.

To make the beurre blanc: Thinly slice carambolas so that they look like stars. Place them in a large saucepot with clementine juice, wine, sugar, and vanilla bean. Cook on low heat for 20 minutes or until the fruit is soft and tender and wine has reduced by one-third. Set aside until ready to serve.

To prepare the fish: Preheat oven to 400°F. Season both sides of the fish with salt and pepper to taste. Heat a cast-iron skillet over high heat until nearly smoking. Add olive oil and gently place the fish in the pan, skin-side down. Place your spatula on the fish to prevent it from curling and to establish an even sear on the skin. Sear the fish for 1 minute, then transfer pan to oven and finish fish for about 3–5 minutes, until fish flakes with a fork. Remove fish from pan, cover, and keep it warm until plating.

To prepare the brassica: While fish is cooking, heat a medium sauté pan over high heat until nearly smoking. Add olive oil and place greens in the pan. Sauté until all leaves are wilted, about 1½ minutes, stirring constantly to prevent burning. Add salt and pepper to taste. Drain greens in a colander.

To finish the beurre blanc and croquettes: Place saucepot of carambolas over low heat. Slowly whisk in butter, a few cubes at a time. Add a squeeze of lime and salt to taste. Pour beurre blanc through a sieve into a clean medium saucepan placed on a warm spot on the stove.

Place ½ inch of vegetable oil in a deep sauté pan over medium-high heat until it shimmers. Working in two batches, fry croquettes, turning once, until golden all over, about 5 minutes. Drain on paper towels and transfer to a platter.

To plate and serve: Place half of the wilted brassica down the center of each dinner plate. Ladle beurre blanc around the brassica. Place a hogfish fillet atop each serving of wilted brassica. Place 3 salt cod croquettes around the fish (1 o'clock, 5 o'clock, 9 o'clock) on the beurre blanc.

Kaiyo Grill

81701 Old Highway, MM-81.7, Oceanside
Islamorada, FL 33036
(305) 664-5556
KAIYOGRILL.COM
Chef Emilio Molina, Executive Sushi Chef

"I had no idea this was going to be my calling," says Kaiyo's executive sushi chef Emilio Molina about his sushi career. Born in Puerto Rico and raised in Kissimmee, Florida, Molina trained in classic French culinary techniques, earning a degree at Le Cordon Bleu in Orlando.

"My first job out of school was salad prep at Kafé Kalik, a Bahamian-style restaurant with a sushi bar," he recalls. His station was next to the sushi bar, where Molina observed the Korean sushi chef, Tuyen Le, making amazing creations. "I would watch every day and see what he was doing," says Molina. "I would come in early, off the clock, and cut vegetables for him, make rice, fold towels, whatever grunt work he wanted me to do, just so I could hang out with him. I owe my sushi career to this man!"

"I like to draw," Molina continues, "and I figured out that the attention to detail that sushi requires is where I would best fit." Molina learned the art of sushi-making from Tuyen Le for a year, and then moved on to other sushi bar restaurants to hone his craft. He joined Kaiyo in 2012. "I did a seven-course sushi-tasting tryout for Bob Rich, Kaiyo's owner, and it was pretty much a shoo-in," he says with a wry smile.

The word *sushi* actually means "vinegared rice" in Japanese, but Molina thinks sushi is in your heart. "It's art," he says. "It's a form of expression. Like an artist would pick up a paint brush, I pick up a sushi knife." "I like to hit all the senses," he goes on, "smell, sight, crunch, salty, sweet, spicy. I like to hit all those notes in my food."

Molina makes all his sauces from scratch and uses a lot of different ingredients. Each day on the way to the restaurant, he stops at his fishmonger in Tavernier Creek and picks up what he wants for that day, fresh off the boat. "I break down all the fish myself," says Molina. "As you grow in your sushi career, that is the last thing you are allowed to do. You need a certain skill level."

Kaiyo also offers vibrant Asian-fused cuisine from the kitchen, but the sushi bar holds center stage. "When I tell people to sit at the sushi bar, it's more like dinner and a movie," he jokes, " because I put on a show for them. I interact with them."

"I eat, sleep, and dream sushi. Making sushi is what I love," he proclaims. "It is an everyday learning process. There are always new things to use, always a new page to turn to make your food that much better. I'm very passionate about what I do." And he is very, very good at it as well!

YELLOWTAIL TIRADITO

(SERVES 1)

Executive sushi chef Emilio Molina explains: "Tiradito is a Peruvian dish of raw fish that is sliced very thin, sometimes flattened, and seasoned with a delicate hand. A lighter version of ceviche without the pungency of the raw onion, tiradito resembles an Italian carpaccio or a Japanese sashimi."

For the ponzu sauce:

1 cup soy sauce
Squeeze of 1 lemon, 1 orange, 1 lime

For the sushi:

1 ounce ponzu sauce
1 teaspoon white truffle oil
6 (½-ounce) fresh Pacific yellowtail medallions (hamachi)
    or any sushi-grade fish of your choice
2 teaspoons goat cheese, molded into 6 small balls
¼ Granny Smith apple, thinly sliced lengthwise
1 teaspoon coarse sea salt
1 jalapeño, thinly sliced into circles
6 cilantro leaves
Sriracha

To make the ponzu sauce: Mix together soy sauce and citrus juices. Place in a covered container and refrigerate until needed. (This makes much more than you need, but it holds a long time in the refrigerator. You can also use commercially bottled ponzu sauce.)

To assemble the sushi: In a small bowl, mix ponzu sauce with white truffle oil. Place 6 Asian soupspoons on a rectangular serving plate. Place just enough truffle ponzu sauce in each to cover the bottom of the spoon.

Place 1 yellowtail medallion in each spoon. Place 1 ball of goat cheese atop each medallion. Place 1 slice of apple atop each ball of goat cheese. Sprinkle each portion with sea salt. Place 1 slice of jalapeño atop each slice of apple and a cilantro leaf atop jalapeño. Lightly dot the fish with Sriracha.

To serve: Each spoonful holds one perfect bite.

Pierre's at Morada Bay

81600 Overseas Highway, MM-81.6, Bayside
Islamorada, FL 33036
(305) 664-3225
PIERRES-RESTAURANT.COM
Jouvens Jean, Executive Chef

The sparkling waters of the Gulf of Mexico . . . Swaying palms peppering a white sandy beach . . . The sun melting into the sea . . . The astonishing vista from the wraparound dining porch of the elegant white plantation house that is Pierre's is matched only by the astonishing résumé of its executive chef, Jouvens Jean, and his amazing cuisine.

Of Haitian descent but Bahamian born and raised in Miami from the age of thirteen, Jean has packed a lot of cooking into his thirty-two years. He credits his first kitchen job in an Italian restaurant in the summer after high school as showing him the "artistic part of food, what food could become." "It kind of set something off in my head," he says.

Jean worked his way up the pecking order in some of the best restaurants in Miami-Dade; earned degrees in hospitality and tourism management from FIU; traveled extensively to such far-flung countries as Peru, Brazil, France, and China; and then won the Food Network's "Chef Wanted" challenge. Turning down his prize—a restaurant in

Spain—Jean instead accepted the offer of Hubert Baudoin, Pierre's owner, to take over the helm as executive chef at the exquisite Pierre's and sister restaurant Morada Bay Beach Cafe.

Given carte blanche to revamp the cuisine, which he describes now as international with a Caribbean nod to his roots, Jean loves the opportunity to dare to be different. "If I step out of the box a little bit, what can I get from that?" he asks himself. "At the end of the day, food is food. A lemon is a lemon. But what can you get out of that lemon that people won't expect coming from a lemon?"

Jean personally travels up to Homestead in search of the best fresh produce, straight from the farms. And he has gardens right at Pierre's. Jean often picks out one ingredient and he and his team will free-associate collaboratively during afternoon prep as to what to do with it. "One time I found purple dragon fruit, which I'd never seen before. We made sauce, relish, compote, sorbet. Specials are spontaneous!"

"This may sound corny," he says with his infectious laugh, "but one of my favorite ingredients is the people I get to work with at Pierre's, because everybody is so different and everybody brings something special to the table. Cooking is the easy part. But to have people who are going to really bring different techniques to the elements brings the whole thing together."

Grilled Octopus with Crispy Capers, Extra-Virgin Olive Oil, Smoked Paprika & Green Pea Tendrils

(SERVES 8 AS AN APPETIZER)

For the octopus:

4 cups water
½ cup salt
½ cup sugar
¼ cup pickling spice
Juice of 4 lemons
4–6 pounds fresh octopus

For the marinade:

1 cup extra-virgin olive oil
1 cup soy sauce
2 tablespoons allspice
2 tablespoons ground or powdered garlic
2 tablespoons onion powder
2 tablespoons Aji Amarillo powder, optional*
2 tablespoons chili powder
2 tablespoons cumin
2 tablespoons Chinese five spice powder

For the fried capers:

10 (small) capers
½ cup olive oil

½ cup green pea tendrils, arugula, or watercress
1 teaspoon smoked paprika
½ cup extra-virgin olive oil
Salt and freshly ground black pepper

To prepare the octopus: Place water, salt, sugar, pickling spice, and lemon juice in a large pot over medium-high heat. Bring this court bouillon to a boil. Dip octopus tentacles and bodies in the boiling court bouillon 3 times, waiting 5 seconds between each dipping. Then submerge each octopus in the bouillon and allow octopus to cook for 45 minutes.

To make the marinade: While octopus is cooking, mix all the marinade ingredients in a medium bowl and set aside until needed.

To prepare the fried capers: Drain capers and pat dry with paper towels. Heat olive oil in a small high-sided saucepan over medium-high heat. Add capers to oil and fry until they are crisp and appear to no longer be frying. Remove capers from oil using a slotted spoon and drain on paper towels. Allow capers to rest at room temperature until needed.

To finish the octopus: Once octopus is cooked through, remove from liquid and cool at room temperature. Once cooled, remove tentacles from bodies. Slice tentacles in long, thin strips and submerge them in the marinade. Set aside in the refrigerator for 4 hours. (**Note:** The rest of the octopus is edible and can be used in other cooking applications, such as for a soup or even chopped into a fresh salad. Place the octopus bodies in a ziplock bag and refrigerate until needed.)

Remove tentacles from the marinade and place them on a hot grill just long enough to get a nice char on each side. (**Note:** Be careful not to put

too many tentacles on the grill at one time, as too much oil from the marinade could cause an oil fire on your grill.)

To plate: Arrange approximately 1 tablespoon green pea tendrils on each of 8 small plates. Place an octopus tentacle atop tendrils. Finish with a sprinkle of smoked paprika and crispy

capers. Drizzle 1 tablespoon extra-virgin olive oil atop each portion and season with a pinch of salt and freshly ground black pepper. Serve immediately.

*Chef Jouvens advises: "Aji Amarillo powder is a Peruvian yellow pepper paste. While it is optional in this recipe, it adds a bit of heat to the dish."

Local Hogfish Meunière with Olive Oil Poached Potatoes, Haricots Verts, and Heirloom Tomato & Parsley Salad

(SERVES 2)

For the potatoes:

8 medium fingerling potatoes
2 cups extra-virgin olive oil
Salt and freshly ground black pepper
2 tablespoons chopped parsley

For the haricots verts:

4 cups water
6 ounces green beans, trimmed
2 tablespoons olive oil
Salt and freshly ground black pepper

For the truffle vinaigrette:

1 cup red wine vinegar
2 teaspoons chopped shallots
1 ounce truffle oil
1 ounce blended oil*

For the heirloom tomato and parsley salad:

½ cup diced heirloom tomatoes
¼ cup truffle vinaigrette
2 tablespoons coarsely chopped parsley
Salt and freshly ground black pepper

For the fish:

¼ cup all-purpose flour
Salt and freshly ground black pepper
2 (6-ounce) hogfish fillets
2 tablespoons clarified butter, divided

For sauce meunière:

4 tablespoons whole butter
2 tablespoons fresh lemon juice
4 teaspoons chopped parsley
Salt

To prepare the potatoes: Wash fingerling potatoes and dry them with paper towels. Place olive oil in a heavy-duty saucepan over medium heat. Add potatoes and cook for about 20 minutes, until fork tender. Remove potatoes from oil and place on an ovenproof plate. Season with salt and pepper to taste. Sprinkle with chopped parsley. Set aside until needed.

To prepare the haricots verts: Bring water to a rapid boil in a medium saucepan. Add beans and cook for 30 seconds. Drain beans and

immediately submerge them in a bowl of ice water to stop the cooking process. Remove beans from ice water and pat them dry with paper towels. Heat olive oil in a 10-inch sauté pan over medium heat. Sauté haricots verts for 15 seconds, then, using a slotted spoon, transfer beans to an ovenproof plate. Season the beans with salt and pepper to taste. Set aside until needed.

To make the truffle vinaigrette: Whisk vinegar, shallots, and oils together in a medium bowl. Set aside until needed.

To make the heirloom tomato and parsley salad: Place tomatoes, vinaigrette, and parsley in a large mixing bowl. Toss to combine. Season with salt and pepper to taste. Set aside until needed.

To prepare the fish: Preheat oven to 350°F. Place flour on a dinner plate and season with salt and pepper to taste. Dredge both sides of hogfish fillets in flour. Place half the clarified butter in a large ovenproof sauté pan over medium heat. When butter is hot, add fillets to pan and cook for about 45 seconds or until they start to turn brown. Flip fillets and cook other sides until fillets brown slightly, about 45 seconds.

Transfer sauté pan to oven and cook fish for 4–5 minutes. (Place the plates of potatoes and haricots verts on the top rack of the oven at this time to warm them.) When fish is flaky and just cooked through, remove sauté pan and the potatoes and haricots verts from oven. Place 1 hogfish fillet onto each dinner plate.

To make the sauce meunière: Place the sauté pan over medium heat and add whole butter to pan. Once butter has melted, add lemon juice and parsley. Cook until butter browns. Add salt to taste.

To plate: Place 4 potatoes and an equal portion of haricots verts alongside hogfish fillet on each dinner plate. Pour sauce meunière over each fillet. Garnish each plate with half the heirloom tomato and parsley salad. Serve immediately.

*Chef Jouvens advises: "Blended oil is 75 percent extra-virgin olive oil and 25 percent canola oil. It is important in this recipe because 100 percent extra-virgin olive oil will change the flavor of the fish."

Morada Bay Beach Cafe

81600 Overseas Highway, MM-81.6, Bayside
Islamorada, FL 33036
(305) 664-0604
MORADABAY-RESTAURANT.COM
Luigi Maestri, Chef de Cuisine

Growing up in Colombia, part of a large Spanish-Italian family, Luigi Maestri loved to cook at an early age. His father was from northern Italy, his mother from the Caribbean coastal side of Colombia, so fusion cooking started in his household long before it became avant-garde. "I used to make like 600 raviolis and cannoli with my Aunt Mirrella before the holidays," he recalls. "I liked to cook. I even took a high school elective in cooking and the guys teased me."

Maestri studied international gastronomy, but the business side of the industry did not intrigue him like the kitchen did. Moving to Costa Rica, a country he loved, Maestri honed his craft and lived *la vida loca* until, in 2004, his wife wanted to move to the States. Because his mother-in-law was here, he moved straight to the Keys, landing a job in the grill station at Pierre's. The owner, Hubert Baudoin, "helped me a lot," he says.

One day the pastry chef quit and the executive chef asked Maestri to take over until they could hire another. "Hey, I've never

worked making desserts, but if you show me, I'll cover until the new guy gets here," he said. That day didn't come for two years, by which time Maestri had mastered the fine art of baking. He went over to Pierre's sister restaurant, Morada Bay Beach Cafe, and quickly worked his way up through the line. In 2011, "Hubert called me and said, 'Luigi, you are the new head chef at Morada Bay," he recalls.

"You can do whatever you want in a kitchen," says Maestri, "but you need balance. Balance of colors, flavors, and textures on the plate is important." And he credits his great kitchen team for maintaining that balance. "Sometimes I turn around and I see the order machine and the long line of tickets just hanging there, and it gets crazy for a while. We might scream a little, but we love the chaos."

Morada Bay Beach Cafe sits on a white powdery imported beach on the shores of Florida Bay. Tall palm trees pepper the sand, punctuated with colorful dining tables and lounging areas with Adirondack chairs. "When you are on the beach and feeling the sand between your toes and seeing the sunset while you are dining, it is amazing!" says Maestri.

Whole Fried Snapper with Tropical Sweet Chili Salsa & Warm Vegetable Slaw

(SERVES 1)

For the mango tropical salsa:

1 cup peeled, diced mango
2 tablespoons diced sweet onions, like Vidalia
1 jalapeño, seeded and diced
5 cloves garlic, minced
Small bunch cilantro, chopped
Juice of 2 limes
Salt

For the sweet chili sauce:

1 ounce crushed red pepper flakes
½ cup brown sugar
1½ cups pineapple juice
1 tablespoon cornstarch
1 tablespoon water

For the snapper:

1 (1¼–1½ pound) cleaned, whole yellowtail snapper
Salt and black pepper
1 cup all-purpose flour
½ cup cornstarch
Vegetable oil for frying

For the warm vegetable slaw:

1 tablespoon olive oil
⅓ cup julienned carrots
⅓ cup julienned yellow squash
⅓ cup julienned zucchini
⅓ cup julienned fennel

To make the mango tropical salsa: Combine mangoes, onions, jalapeños, and garlic in a medium mixing bowl. Stir in cilantro and lime juice. Add salt to taste. Transfer to a covered container and refrigerate until needed.

To make the sweet chili sauce: Place crushed red pepper flakes, brown sugar, and pineapple juice in a medium saucepan over medium-high heat. Bring to a boil. Mix cornstarch and water in a small bowl to form a slurry. Stir slurry into pineapple mixture and stir until thickened. Cover and keep sauce warm on low heat.

To prepare the snapper: Score fish with diagonal cuts on both sides. Season both sides of the fish with salt and pepper to taste. Mix flour and cornstarch on a large plate. Dredge fish in mixture. Place enough oil in a large, heavy sauté pan so that it will come halfway up the side of the fish. Heat oil in pan over medium-high heat. Add fish and fry for 4 minutes per side or until cooked through.

To make the slaw: While fish is frying, place olive oil in a medium sauté pan over medium heat. Add julienned carrots, squash, zucchini, and fennel and sauté until just al dente. Set aside.

To assemble: Place vegetables in the center of a dinner plate. Lay fish atop vegetables. Mix ½ cup warm sweet chili sauce with mango tropical salsa. Place warm salsa alongside the fish. Drizzle sweet chili sauce atop the fish. Serve immediately.

Islamorada Fish Company

81532 Overseas Highway, MM-81.5, Bayside
Islamorada, FL 33036
(800) 258-2559
IFCSTONECRAB.COM

An iconic staple on the Islamorada landscape for decades, Islamorada Fish Company started out in 1948 as a family-run commercial fishery and cooking shack. Dorothy and George Hertel took over the business in the 1980s and added a small restaurant to the fish company. Then, in 1998, Bass Pro Shops founder Johnny Morris, who had vacationed in the Keys for twenty-five years, bought the Fish Company and put the place on the map.

At that time still primarily a fish market selling the fresh catch of a fleet of local fishermen, Islamorada Fish Company, which sits on the shore of Florida Bay, began serving simple fresh fish and seafood baskets to diners seated at umbrella-topped tables. The restaurant became so popular that it was not unusual to have to wait an hour and a half for a table. (Morris then bought the Green Turtle Cannery next door and converted it to be the stand-alone wholesale/retail fish market, and purchased property on the other side of Islamorada Fish Company and opened the cavernous fishing emporium, World Wide Sportsman.)

Hurricane Wilma gets credit for the Islamorada Fish Company restaurant of today. The hurricane damaged the property to the extent that it required rebuilding. Now "sittin' on the dock of the bay" beneath a giant tiki hut adjacent to a natural tarpon pool, the restaurant still serves its famous Islamorada Fish Company Sandwich as well as a bevy of other fresh fish and seafood brought in daily to the fish market by the five or so boats in their fleet.

And while this, "the original" Islamorada Fish Company is part of the Bass Pro Shops empire (sister restaurants are cloned in more than a dozen inland locations across the United States) and its recipes are developed in their Midwest corporate kitchens, the restaurant retains the charm it has always exuded: The fish is fresh. The atmosphere, lively. And the sunsets are spectacular.

Fresh Catch-of-the-Day
with Shrimp Portofino Sauce

(SERVES 4)

For the catch-of-the-day:

1 tablespoon butter
4 (6–8 ounce) fresh fish fillets
Salt and freshly ground black pepper

For the shrimp Portofino sauce:

1 tablespoon butter
12 large (20–25s) shrimp, peeled and deveined,
    tails left on
½ shallot, minced
2 ounces brandy
1 cup heavy cream
1 tablespoon flour
1 teaspoon seafood seasoning or Old Bay Seasoning

2 tablespoons snipped fresh parsley

To prepare the catch of the day: Warm grill until hot or preheat oven to 350°F. Place 1 tablespoon butter in a small glass dish and microwave until butter is melted, about 15 seconds. Baste fish fillets on both sides with butter and season them with salt and pepper to taste. Place fish on hot grill or into oven in an ovenproof baking pan. Grill or bake fillets until they are opaque and flake lightly when tested with a fork (or reach 145°F when tested with an instant-read food thermometer).

To make the shrimp Portofino sauce: Meanwhile, melt 1 tablespoon butter in a large sauté pan over medium heat. Add shrimp and sauté for 1–2 minutes, stirring frequently. (Take care not to burn butter.) Add shallots and cook until translucent. Add brandy to deglaze pan and reduce it by half. Add cream and continue cooking until sauce is reduced by one-quarter. Add flour and stir continuously until thickened. Stir in seafood seasoning. Reduce heat to low and allow sauce to cook for 5 minutes.

To plate and serve: Place a fish fillet in the center of each of 4 dinner plates. Spoon one-quarter of shrimp Portofino sauce atop each serving. Garnish each portion with ½ tablespoon snipped parsley. Serve immediately

Yankees may boast about their blue crabs and West Coasters about Dungeness, but here in the Florida Keys, stone crabs reign supreme. These large non-swimming crabs found in deep holes and under rocks in the waters surrounding the Keys sport two porcelain-like claws, the crusher and the ripper. The crab uses its larger claw, the crusher, to fight predators and to hold its food in place, while the smaller, thinner claw, the ripper, cuts its prey like scissors.

The stone crab possesses the unusual ability to regenerate a severed appendage. Therefore, by Florida law, when harvesting stone crabs from their baited traps, fishermen must remove the claws and return the crabs back to the sea. "If you put pressure on the claw in the right way, the crab will release it for you," says stone crab researcher Randy Hochberg. "If you force it, the claw breaks down near the body, the wound won't heal, and the crab will likely die." The stone crab will fully grow back its claws within eighteen months, a feat it can accomplish three or four times during its lifetime.

In-season from October to May, stone crab claws have long been considered a delicacy in the Florida Keys. Because icing or freezing a raw stone crab claw causes the meat to stick to the inside of the shell, the fresh claws are immediately cooked after harvest. A mild, sweet odor indicates freshness; any hint of ammonia means the cooked crab claws are old. Usually served cold with mustard sauce or reheated with key lime butter, stone crab claws must be cracked with a wooden mallet before the succulent meat can be extracted.

And like any treasure of the realm, stone crab claws—ranging from $20 to $40 per pound—might just be worth their weight in gold!

Green Turtle Inn

81219 Overseas Highway, MM-81.2, Oceanside
Islamorada, FL 33036
(305) 664-2006
GREENTURTLEINN.COM
Chris Visger, Executive Chef

Sid and Roxie Siderious opened the Green Turtle Inn in 1947, and it quickly became a haven of good food, good music, and good times for local fishermen and travelers alike. Green sea turtles were a staple on the menu back then, served as steaks or in soups and chowders. The couple also opened Sid & Roxie's Cannery across the street, where they canned their green turtle soup for decades.

Nowhere is the old adage "The more things change, the more things stay the same" more true than at the Green Turtle. Sid and Roxie are long gone, as is the cannery (now Islamorada Fish Company Market). Green turtles no longer can be harvested in Keys waters by law. But good food, good music, and good times prevail at the beautifully renovated Islamorada landmark, where a loyal contingent of locals and tourists gather and dine every day except Monday, when "the Turtle rests."

"Our signature dish is still turtle soup," says executive chef Chris Visger, "but now we use wild-caught Louisiana snapping turtles." Raised in Virginia, Visger joined the Green Turtle culinary team in 2011, after an eight-year stint at Richmond's five-star Lemaire restaurant in the historic Jefferson Hotel. "Green Turtle has the center-of-a-small-town feel to it," he says. "It's been here so long."

A graduate of Virginia Tech with a double major in history and hospitality as well as a culinary degree from the Scottsdale (Arizona) Culinary Institute, Visger describes his cuisine as casual fine dining that combines Southern flavors with classic French techniques. "Got to have some pork, bacon, and brown sugar in there," he laughs.

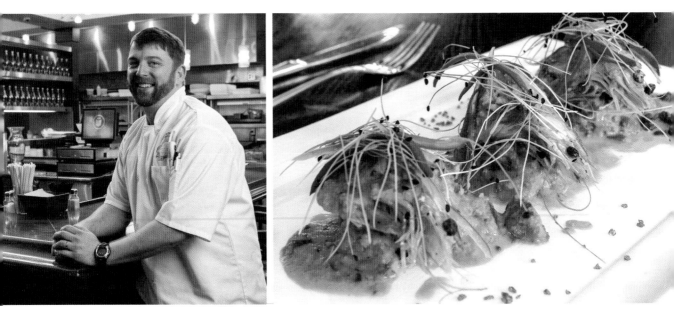

Visger was attracted to cooking because of the creative outlet it presents. "Yep, it's not about the money!" he jokes. "I have a pretty decent palate, and I know kind of what flavors will work with each other," he says when explaining how he goes about creating a new dish for the Turtle. "I keep a pad and pencil next to my bed, and I jot down the ideas as they come to me." He adds, "A lot of the dishes I'm doing nowadays don't have a starch in them because of people's dietary restrictions. I'll do a couple of vegetables or add a secondary protein instead."

"I try to keep a real level head when things get crazy in the kitchen because that is when the team needs to look to their chef for guidance, for a calming influence," says Visger. "Being a chef is like being a teacher or a coach. You are teaching people every day how to do things. I like that aspect of it."

Shrimp Sliders

(SERVES 4)

For the tomato-fennel sauce:

8 Roma tomatoes, diced
2 cups clam juice
1 bulb fennel, diced
Pinch of red pepper flakes
Salt and freshly ground black pepper

For the Parmesan grit cakes:

1½ cups grits (not instant)
1 tablespoon butter
1 cup shredded Parmesan cheese
Salt and freshly ground black pepper

For the shrimp sauté:

1 tablespoon butter
1 red bell pepper, cut brunoise*
1 green bell pepper, cut brunoise*
2 smoked chorizo sausages, cut in small dice
2 cloves garlic, minced
12 (U-12) jumbo shrimp, cleaned and deveined
½ cup white wine
2 tablespoons heavy cream

For the garnishes:

1 red bell pepper, julienned
1 green bell pepper julienned
Micro greens, chives, or chopped scallions

To make the sauce: Place diced tomatoes, clam juice, fennel, and red pepper flakes in a medium saucepan over medium-high heat. Bring to a boil, stirring occasionally. Reduce heat to low and simmer for 1 hour. Carefully puree with an immersion blender or transfer to a blender and puree. Season with salt and pepper to taste. Set aside until needed.

To make the grit cakes: Bring a quart of water to a boil in a large saucepan. Slowly stir in grits and butter. Continue stirring until grits bloom, about 5 minutes. (If you use instant grits, follow package instructions for cooking.) Add cheese and stir until it is incorporated. Add salt and pepper to taste. Spread grits onto a baking sheet in a thin, even layer. Allow grits to cool. Cut grits into 2-inch-round cakes with a cookie cutter. (You'll need 12 cakes.)

To make the shrimp sauté: Melt butter is a large sauté pan over high heat. Add peppers, sausage, and garlic and sauté for 2 minutes, stirring occasionally. Add shrimp and cook 1 minute more. Add wine to deglaze pan. When wine has reduced by three-quarters, add reserved tomato-fennel sauce. When shrimp have turned pink and are just cooked through, stir in cream and remove from heat.

To assemble: Place 3 grit cakes on each of 4 appetizer-size plates. Place 1 shrimp atop each cake. Spoon sauté sauce over each shrimp. Garnish with julienned bell peppers and micro greens.

*Brunoise is a precision culinary knife cut in which the food is first julienned (cut into thin matchsticks), then turned a quarter turn and diced again, thus producing tiny cubes with equal sides.

Lobster-Stuffed Squash Blossom Salad

(SERVES 4–6)

For the squash blossoms:

½ pound lobster meat, cut into small dice
2 cups cream cheese, softened
Pinch of cayenne pepper
2 avocados, diced
Salt and freshly ground black pepper
18 squash blossoms

For the salad:

6 ears sweet corn
2 tablespoons olive oil, divided
2 jalapeños, seeded and cut brunoise*
1 pint grape tomatoes
1 watermelon radish, peeled and thinly sliced
3 cups watermelon balls
1 jalapeño, thinly sliced

For the sweet corn cream:

Reserved corncobs
32 ounces heavy cream
Salt and freshly ground black pepper

For the tempura:

2 cups all-purpose flour
Pinch of baking powder
¾ cup cornstarch
32 ounces club soda
Salt and freshly ground black pepper

To assemble the squash blossoms: Combine lobster, cream cheese, cayenne pepper, and avocados in a large mixing bowl. Season with salt and black pepper to taste. Transfer mixture to a pastry bag with a large metal tip (#6). Pipe stuffing into each squash blossom. Transfer blossoms to a large plate, cover with plastic wrap, and refrigerate until needed.

To make the salad: Preheat oven to 350°F. Brush corn with oil and place it directly on the oven rack. Place a baking sheet underneath the corn to catch the drippings. Roast corn in the oven until soft and tender, about 10–12 minutes. Cut kernels off cobs, reserving cobs. Combine corn and brunoise-cut jalapeños in a medium bowl. Stir to mix. Refrigerate until needed.

Increase oven temperature to 400°F. Brush grape tomatoes with olive oil and place on a baking sheet. Roast them in the oven just until they start to blister. Remove tomatoes from oven and slip off their skins. Refrigerate until needed.

To make the sweet corn cream: Cut reserved corncobs into thirds. Place in a large saucepan and add cream. Simmer over low to medium heat until cream has reduced by half. Season with salt and pepper to taste. Remove from heat and refrigerate until needed.

To make the tempura: Place flour, baking powder, and cornstarch in a large bowl. Slowly whisk in the club soda until the consistency resembles pancake batter. Season with salt and pepper to taste.

To cook the squash blossoms: Working in small batches, dip each filled squash blossom into tempura batter and carefully place in deep-fat fryer. Fry squash blossoms until they are golden brown. Transfer fried squash blossoms to a platter lined with paper towels.

To assemble the salad: Divide corn mixture among 4 to 6 plates, mounding it in the middle of the plate. Top corn with 3 or 4 squash blossoms. Place radishes so that they are sticking out of the corn. Scatter watermelon balls, tomatoes, and jalapeño slices around the plate. Remove corncobs from corn cream and drizzle cooled corn cream over entire salad. Serve immediately.

*Brunoise is a precision culinary knife cut where the food is first julienned (cut into thin matchsticks), then turned a quarter turn and diced again, thus producing tiny cubes with equal sides.

Spanish Gardens Cafe

80925 Overseas Highway, MM-80.9, Oceanside
Islamorada, FL 33036
(305) 664-3999
SPANISHGARDENSCAFE.COM
Jose Palomino, Chef and Owner

Jose Palomino does not consider himself a chef. "Mother Nature is our chef," he says. Born and raised in the Basque region of Spain, Palomino believes in using only the highest-quality ingredients in his made-from-scratch-before-your-eyes cuisine at Spanish Gardens.

So, while demonstrating how to prepare salmorejo—the rich, smooth gazpacho typical of that served in Cordoba, Spain—Palomino instructs: "The finest ingredients are essential to this recipe. Use only fresh, flavorful summer tomatoes or, in other seasons, try 'ugly,' heirloom, or vintage tomatoes. French sea salt imparts a different flavor than other sea salts. The sherry should be imported from the south of Spain. And make sure extra-virgin olive oil is first-pressed and estate bottled. The results are worth the extra money and effort!"

As a youth, Palomino attended a Catholic boarding school for eleven years. Because of his family's poverty, he attended for free, but from the time he was seven years old, he was required to work in the school's kitchen when not in class. "Can you imagine picking little stones out of a hundred pounds of lentils?" he asks.

From school he went to work in his brother-in-law's restaurant kitchen, which he says "was filled with mean, picky people!" But he learned the quality of ingredients and to be meticulous in his cooking. In need of a change, he vacationed in the Florida Keys in 1981, met his wife Teddy, and, like so many before him, stayed.

"I didn't want to cook anymore," he says, "so I decided to be a commercial fisherman. I didn't have a clue how to fish, but when I got a glimpse of fishermen drinking at Marathon's Brass Monkey until 2 a.m., I thought, 'How hard can it be?'" Palomino harvested lobsters and stone crabs for twelve years before hanging up his traps and returning to cooking. "What else I can do [*sic*]?" he says with his still-heavy Basque accent.

His successful ventures—Garden Gourmet in Marathon and Garden Cafe in the Rain Barrel in Islamorada—preceded his opening Spanish Gardens Cafe in 2007. He cooks authentic Basque dishes with an island twist, tapas style. "To us, tapas are not a particular food or style of food, but rather a way of eating, a lifestyle of sharing," says Palomino. He adds, "Everything must be fresh or I don't serve it that day."

Salmorejo with Shrimp, Avocado & Serrano Ham

(SERVES 6; MAKES 9 CUPS)

For the salmorejo:

6 vine-ripened summer, vintage, or heirloom tomatoes
2 cloves garlic, chopped
1 (6-inch) ciabatta roll, cut into bite-size pieces
2 teaspoons French sea salt
¼ cup aged sherry vinegar (south of Spain)
1 cup estate-bottled extra-virgin olive oil

For the shrimp:

3 cups water
2 lemon wedges
2 bay leaves
6 sprigs flat-leaf parsley
30 large shrimp, shells on

For the garnishes:

8 tablespoons extra-virgin olive oil, divided
9 thin slices Serrano ham, cut in half
3 ripe avocados
24 sprigs arugula

To make the salmorejo: The day before: Core tomatoes and cut them into wedges. Place tomatoes, garlic, ciabatta pieces, and salt in a covered non-metal container. Place vinegar in a medium bowl and slowly whisk in olive oil. Pour over tomato mixture and toss to combine. Cover container and refrigerate overnight.

Transfer tomato mixture to a food processor in batches and process until smooth. (Mixture will be slightly lumpy.) Transfer to a large non-metal container. Working in batches, press tomato mixture through a food mill. Transfer to a clean covered container and refrigerate until well chilled, at least 2 hours.

To prepare the shrimp: Place water, lemon wedges, bay leaves, and parsley in a medium saucepan over high heat. When water comes to a boil, add shrimp and cook until pink, 3–4 minutes. Remove from heat, drain shrimp, and immediately plunge them in an ice water bath. Peel shrimp and discard vegetables. Refrigerate shrimp until needed.

To prepare the garnishes: Place 2 tablespoons olive oil in a medium skillet over medium heat. When oil is hot, add ham and fry until crispy. Remove ham from skillet and drain on paper towels.

Cut each avocado in half. Remove seeds and peel avocados. Cut each avocado half into a 7-section fan, keeping the base portion intact.

To assemble and serve: Place 1½ cups salmorejo in each of 6 large, shallow soup bowls. Place an avocado fan in the center of each portion of soup. Arrange 5 shrimp atop the soup at even intervals around the perimeter of the bowl. Place 3 crispy ham slices upright in the soup around the avocado fan. Place an arugula leaf between each shrimp. Drizzle each portion with 1 tablespoon extra-virgin olive oil and serve immediately.

CHOCOLATE VALENCIA

(SERVES 6–7)

For the Valencia:

6 Valencia oranges
1 cup sugar
2 tablespoons Grand Marnier

For the ganache:

1 pound good semisweet chocolate (70%)
2 tablespoons cultured butter
2 cups heavy cream

For the topping:

2 cups heavy cream
2 tablespoons powdered sugar
1 teaspoon vanilla

To prepare the Valencia: Grate peel of 1 orange and set orange zest aside for later use. Peel the pith and section the orange. Peel and section 4 more oranges, discarding peels. Cut the 1 remaining orange (peel on) in sections. Discard all seeds.

Place oranges in a large saucepan over medium heat. Stir in sugar. When sugar has dissolved, reduce heat to low. Cook for 1 hour, stirring occasionally. Add Grand Marnier and continue cooking oranges for 15 more minutes, until most of the liquid has evaporated.

Transfer to a blender and pulse until smooth. Allow orange mixture to cool. Place about ⅓ cup orange mixture into the bottom of 6 or 7 wine or martini glasses. Refrigerate at least 1 hour, until chilled.

To prepare the ganache: Coarsely chop chocolate. Melt butter in the top of a double boiler over medium heat. Add chocolate and cream and heat, stirring constantly, until chocolate is melted and mixture is smooth. Place about ⅓ cup chocolate mixture atop orange mixture in each of the glasses. Cover glasses with plastic wrap and refrigerate until needed.

To make the topping: Place cream in the bowl of an electric mixer. Whip cream on medium speed until thickened. Add powdered sugar and vanilla and whip just until soft peaks form.

To serve: Top each Chocolate Valencia with about 2 tablespoonfuls of whipped cream. Top each serving with a sprinkling of the reserved grated orange peel.

Lazy Days

79867 Overseas Highway, MM-79.8, Oceanside
Islamorada, FL 33036
(305) 664-5256
LAZYDAYSRESTAURANT.COM
Lupe Ledesma, Chef and Owner

Chef Lupe Ledesma came directly to the Keys from his native Mexico in 1986 at the age of sixteen, sponsored by an uncle who got him a job as a busboy at the Italian Fisherman. "The language barrier was too much for me; I couldn't speak English," exclaims Lupe. "I would hide in the bathroom and cry." Requesting a position washing dishes in the safe haven of the kitchen, he learned English and worked his way up the line.

Cooking at Perry's, the Quay, and Squid Row in the Upper Keys, Ledesma developed a following of loyal customers who loved his food and followed him wherever his apron took him. "I was fortunate enough to work with some great chefs and absorb a little bit here and there and then come up with my own things," he says.

In 2002 Ledesma and his wife, Michelle, acquired Lazy Days, an expansive dining room on stilts perched directly on the shores of the Atlantic Ocean. With that view and Ledesma's magic in the kitchen, it is no wonder that there are days when by 2:00 p.m. they already have 200 reservations.

Ledesma's philosophy: "Keep it simple! I just want to do what the customer wants." And although Lazy Days has an expansive menu of land-based offerings, what the customers here usually want is for Chef Lupe to cook the fish they caught that day. "In season, more than 175 customers a night bring in their own fish," he says. "We label it with name and table number so there's no mix-up. It's a lot of labor for the kitchen team, but it is worth it."

Ledesma crowns the simply sautéed catch-of-the-day with special key lime butter-based preparations he calls "toppings." "We have a master book with about 500 topping recipes," he says. "Cooking is like music," he goes on. "There is always a new way to put the notes together." And his culinary team will put each table's catch together with up to six different toppings, serving it family-style on a giant platter. Lazy Days Style ranks as the hands-down favorite and is upstaged only by the mini loaf of fresh banana bread that starts every meal.

Surrounded by a sea of great food, day in and day out, Ledesma sheepishly confesses that his favorite at-home meal is Hamburger Helper and mashed potatoes. "Pretty much at home I just do the dishes!" he jokes.

Hogfish Tropical

(SERVES 4)

For the tropical sauce:

2 sticks butter, divided
½ cup diced papaya
½ cup diced mango
½ cup diced pineapple
1 banana, sliced
¼ cup dry-toasted coconut flakes
½ cup coconut rum
½ cup heavy cream

For the fish fillets:

3 eggs
½ cup all-purpose flour
2 pounds hogfish fillets
2 tablespoons margarine or canola oil
2 tablespoons snipped fresh parsley

To make the tropical sauce: Place 4 tablespoons butter in a medium sauté pan over medium-high heat. Add papaya, mango, pineapple, bananas, and coconut and sauté for about 1 minute. Add rum and flambé, stirring constantly until alcohol has burned off. Reduce heat to medium and reduce sauce by half.

Add remaining butter, 2 tablespoons at a time. When all the butter has melted, stir in cream. Simmer until sauce has thickened, about 1 minute. Remove from heat, cover sauté pan, and place on a warming tray or a warm spot on the stove. (If the sauce separates, stir in a teaspoon or so of water.)

To prepare the fish fillets: Whisk eggs in a large shallow dish. Place flour in a separate large shallow dish. Dredge both sides of fish fillets in flour then dip both sides in the egg wash, making sure the entire fillet is covered. Heat margarine or oil in a large nonstick sauté pan over medium-high heat. Place fillets in pan and cook for 5 minutes or until undersides are golden. Gently turn fillets and cook for 5 minutes more.

To plate and serve: Divide hogfish fillets equally among 4 dinner plates. Top each with an equal portion of tropical sauce, sprinkle with parsley, and serve immediately.

Marathon High School Culinary Program

350 SOMBRERO BEACH ROAD
MARATHON, FL 33050
(305) 289-2480
CHEF CARL STANTON, INSTRUCTOR

The most popular elective at Marathon High School, the culinary arts program is like the Culinary Institute of America or Johnson & Wales for teens. Taught by Chef Carl Stanton, who led many a prestigious kitchen in his more than twenty-five years in the hospitality industry, the program takes the students through a rigorous four-year culinary journey that primes them for a food-and-beverage-oriented career.

Stanton teaches in a state-of-the-art stainless-steel kitchen that most restaurants would covet. Students first learn the basics of good sanitation, accident prevention, proper measurement of ingredients, and, importantly, knife techniques. As they move through the program learning to prepare the five "mother sauces," soups, stocks, and preparation techniques in the kitchen, they are also taught the service end of the business in Dolphin Bistro, the culinary program's very own sixty-seat, ocean-view restaurant, right in the high school.

Built by local design-building firm D'Asign Source and interior designer Liz Samess, Dolphin Bistro resembles an upscale, crystal-and-linen city bistro, with inlaid faux travertine and wood-plank flooring, natural woven shades, and two-color faux-finished walls. Third- and fourth-year students present themed multicourse dinners here, open twice a month to the public, as a means to get real, practical restaurant experience.

The students pick their theme and, taking color, contrast, and taste into consideration, vote on menu items one month ahead of an event. They learn to figure out how much food to order, compute food costs, compare prices from vendors, and check the products when they come in the door. The kitchen brigade researches recipes from the world's

great cuisines and converts them for the bistro dinner. They make a prep list and watch Chef Stanton demonstrate how to prepare the dishes and plate them properly. They choose their roles—dietician, pastry chef, sous chef, grill station, expo, food runners.

The front-of-the-house students maintain the table linens and server uniforms, set up the dining room, and learn how to take orders and serve by position number, as well as how to enhance a patron's dining experience through eye contact and interaction. Chef Stanton conducts his culinary program like a business, with the same disciplinary structure found in a professional restaurant. In other words, "No fooling around!"

In January 2014 Stanton's chefs-in-training competed against the executive chefs from fourteen of the top Florida Keys restaurants in the annual Master Chef's Classic in Key West (see sidebar on pages 168–169). They had to make 425 individual small portions of their recipes for the judges and attendees. The judges tasted, voted, and awarded the students a third-place victory in the dessert category for their Key Lime Parfait. Watch out, Food Network, here they come!

Key Lime Parfait

(SERVES 5)

8 ounces sweetened condensed milk

4 egg yolks

1 cup key lime juice

2 cups heavy cream

2 tablespoons confectioners' sugar

1 tablespoon vanilla extract

½ cup graham cracker crumbs

Whisk condensed milk and egg yolks together in a large bowl. Whisk in key lime juice until mixture has thickened into a custard.

Place heavy cream in the large bowl of an electric mixer. Whip cream on medium speed, increasing the speed as the cream thickens. Add confectioners' sugar and vanilla. Whip until you have soft peaks. (Do not over-whip unless you want butter!)

Build parfait in a 10-ounce martini glass, alternating ½-inch-thick layers of custard and whipped cream (4 to 6 layers), ending with whipped cream. Sprinkle graham cracker crumbs over the top and refrigerate until ready to serve.

Miso Braised Pork Belly & Key Lime–Chili Seared Sea Scallops over Risotto

(SERVES 6)

For the pork belly:

1 pound pork belly, rinsed in cold water
½ cup miso paste
1 cup rice vinegar or mirin
1 tablespoon sambal or chili paste
2 tablespoons low-sodium soy sauce
½ sweet onion, like Vidalia, coarsely chopped
4 cloves garlic, coarsely chopped
Splash of water
1 tablespoon canola oil

For the risotto:

3–4 cups chicken stock
2 large pinches saffron
Extra-virgin olive oil
1 large sweet onion, cut into ¼-inch dice
Kosher salt
2 cups arborio rice
1½–2 cups dry white wine
2 tablespoons butter
½–¾ cup grated Parmigiano-Reggiano

For the scallops:

3 tablespoons chili powder
1 tablespoon white pepper
2 tablespoons kosher salt
12 (U-12) dry diver scallops, washed
    and patted dry
4 tablespoons clarified butter
2 ounces key lime juice
6 tablespoons whole butter
Salt and freshly ground black pepper

To prepare the pork belly: Preheat oven to 350°F. Place pork belly in a large braising pan. Whisk miso paste, vinegar, sambal, soy sauce, onions, garlic, and a splash of water in a medium bowl. Pour mixture over pork belly. Cover pan, place in oven, and braise pork belly for 1½ hours, until belly is soft and you are able to insert a knife through the center with ease.

Remove pan from oven and allow pork belly to cool in the juices. (Braising can be done a day or two ahead of time. Simply cover and refrigerate pork belly. It can also be wrapped and frozen.) Once the belly has cooled, remove it from the pan and cut it into 1-inch cubes. Reserve cooking liquid. Refrigerate pork belly in a covered container until needed.

To make the pork belly sauce: Strain the reserved cooking liquid and put into a saucepan over medium-high heat. Simmer the liquid until it is reduced by half. Refrigerate in a covered container until needed.

To make the risotto: Place chicken stock in a medium saucepan over high heat. Bring to a boil, then reduce heat to medium-low to keep stock hot. Whisk saffron into stock. (Stock should turn bright yellow.)

Place a large saucepan over medium heat. Add enough olive oil to cover the bottom of the pan. Add onions and salt to taste, and sweat the onions until translucent, about 5 minutes. Increase heat to medium-high. Add rice and cook for 3–4 minutes, allowing rice to stick slightly to the bottom of the pan and then scraping it off. (Rice should sound crackly.)

Add enough wine to the pan to cover the surface of the rice. Season with salt to taste and cook, stirring continuously, until wine has absorbed into the rice. Add enough saffron chicken stock to pan until it just covers the rice. Cook, stirring continuously, until stock has absorbed into the rice. Repeat this process two more times with the hot saffron chicken stock. When the stock has been absorbed and the rice is creamy, taste a couple of grains of rice to be sure it is cooked perfectly. If it is still a little crunchy, add a little more stock and cook the rice for another couple of minutes. When perfect to the bite, remove rice from heat. Stir in the butter and Parmigiano-Reggiano.

To prepare the scallops: Mix chili powder, pepper, and salt in a small bowl. Sprinkle both sides of scallops with seasoning to taste. Place a large sauté pan over high heat and add clarified butter. Place scallops in pan and sauté for about 2–3 minutes per side, until nicely seared and just cooked through. Remove scallops and pour off excess butter. Reduce heat to medium-high. Add key lime juice to deglaze the pan. Whisk in the whole butter and season with salt and pepper to taste. Return scallops to pan and coat them with the key lime butter sauce.

To finish the pork belly: While scallops are cooking, place canola oil a large sauté pan over medium-high heat. When oil is hot, place 12 pork belly cubes in pan. Sear for about 3 minutes per side. Remove from heat.

To assemble and serve: Place reserved pork belly sauce in a small saucepan over medium heat. Divide risotto among 6 dinner plates. Top each serving with 2 scallops and 2 pieces of pork belly. Drizzle a little key lime butter sauce over the scallops and a little pork belly sauce over the pork belly cubes for each portion. Serve immediately.

PLAZA GRILL

5101 OVERSEAS HIGHWAY, MM-50, OCEANSIDE
MARATHON, FL 33050
(305) 743-7874
PLAZAGRILLFLKEYS.COM
WILLIAM HUNT, EXECUTIVE CHEF

"I'm in what I call the '40-40 Club,'" says William Hunt with a laugh. "I've been involved in forty restaurants in forty years, in one position or another!" Call him a rolling stone, perhaps, or a member of the brotherhood of traveling knives. "I decided early on to spend only a year at any one restaurant to maximize the education end of it," he says.

While in high school, Hunt completed a four-year culinary program, which placed him in apprenticeships at several Boston restaurants during his junior and senior years. From there he went directly to Boston College, then Emerson College, as a cook. Hopscotching from restaurant to restaurant, working his way up the line in the culinary-

rich city, Hunt honed his craft before finally hanging up his snow shovel and moving to Key West in 1988.

He landed at the Marquesa Hotel, then Louie's Backyard, and even opened his own restaurant, Queen's Table, for a time. He worked his way up the Keys, with stints at Mangrove Mama's, Boondocks, and others, as well as seasonal gigs as a private chef in Alaska and at various fishing camps.

"I'm an ingredients-driven chef," says Hunt. "I enjoy procuring the products as much as I like cooking them." In October 2013 Hunt became executive chef at Plaza Grill in Marathon, which had gotten off to a rocky start in 2012. "It's a flamboyantly elegant facility," he says, with lots of marble, rich cherry and mahogany woods, a granite bar, and lots of glass and brass. "It looks a little like a men's club or a speakeasy right out of Manhattan," he says.

Hunt wanted to create a cuisine at Plaza Grill worthy of its sophisticated surroundings. "Seafood's my bag," says Hunt. "A steak is a steak is a steak." And although he provides stellar steak offerings that more than satisfy carnivores, Hunt—the chef who loves change—likes the creativity a large offering of specials affords him. "The specials are a blend of things I've done before that I love. I like to use ingredients at the pinnacle of freshness, and I'm always pushing it," he says.

"I like when it's really busy and the place is full," says Hunt, "and you can hear people laughing as you're preparing the food just right." "It's like a Broadway show," he continues. "Every night is a performance." It appears Hunt may have put away his culinary track shoes for a while, because he adds, "I want to make Plaza Grill the very best that it can be."

Whole Roasted Yellowtail
with Asian Vegetables, Jasmine Rice
& Ginger Soy Vinaigrette

(SERVES 4)

For the vinaigrette:

2 tablespoons chopped scallions
½ teaspoon orange zest
¼ cup orange juice
¼ cup balsamic vinegar
1 tablespoon minced garlic
¼ cup canola oil
¼ cup sesame oil
1 tablespoon Chinese chili paste
¼ cup soy sauce
1 teaspoon crushed red pepper
1 heaping tablespoon snipped fresh cilantro
¼ cup grated gingerroot
1 tablespoon chopped lemongrass
Juice of 2 key limes

For the fish:

4 (1½–2 pound) yellowtail snappers, scaled,
    gilled, and cleaned
½ cup white wine
½ cup freshly squeezed orange juice
4 cups warm cooked jasmine rice
4 lime wedges
Wasabi
Sriracha

For the vegetables:

1 tablespoon sesame oil
4 cups julienned or chopped mixed Asian vegetables*
Splash of sherry wine

To make the vinaigrette: Place all the ingredients in a blender and pulse until smooth. Reserve ¼ cup vinaigrette for plating. Set the rest aside until needed.

To prepare the yellowtail: Remove all the bones from each fish, except the heads and tails. Place fish in a large nonreactive baking pan and pour vinaigrette over fish. Refrigerate and allow fish to marinate for 2–3 hours.

To prepare the vegetables: Place sesame oil in a large sauté pan over high heat. When oil is hot, add vegetables and sauté until they are crunch-tender. Stir in a splash of sherry and remove from heat.

To cook the yellowtail: Preheat oven to 400°F. Remove fish from marinade. Stuff the cavity of each fish with vegetables and place in a roasting pan in the upright swimming position. (Use skewers if necessary to keep stuffed vegetables inside of fish.) Mix white wine and orange juice in a small bowl and pour into the bottom of the pan. Roast fish for 20–30 minutes (depending on the size of the fish), until fish flakes when tested with a fork.

To plate and serve: Place 1 cup jasmine rice in the center of each dinner plate. Using a long spatula, slide spatula under the fish, being careful not to displace the inside vegetables, and nestle fish atop the rice in the same swimming position. Drizzle 1 tablespoon reserved vinaigrette over each fish. Garnish each serving with a wedge of lime, a bit of wasabi, and a splash of Sriracha.

*Suggested vegetables: napa cabbage, red bell peppers, bok choy, carrots, shiitake mushrooms, jicama, Euro cucumbers, broccolini, and/or scallions.

Barracuda Grill

Enticed to the Keys by the weather, forsaking their frigid homelands of Wisconsin and Illinois, the Hill duo met in Key West in 1988. Jan, a recent Culinary Institute of America graduate, was hired to open the new Hyatt Resort. Lance was fresh out of the US Navy. Fast-forward a few years, and you'll find them married and working side-by-side in the kitchen of their popular Marathon restaurant, Barracuda Grill, where Jan's technical training is matched by Lance's military eye for detail.

"Printing a new menu every night allows us to keep up with our customers' changing tastes, to offer things seasonally, and it allows us the freedom to act upon whimsy. If we want shrimp and grits on the menu, *bam!*, it's on the menu," Lance says. And, he advises: "The voodoo stew recipe allows complete freedom to substitute any and all ingredients with whatever is available; i.e., local fresh seafood and vegetables. Even the addition of Andouille sausage kicks it up a bit!"

A virtual reef of barracuda art, many by local artists, punctuates the walls of the restaurant, which is housed in a sixty-year-old vintage building. The Hills try to add a new piece every year, and while none of the art is officially for sale, "Everything has a price!" Lance says.

Collaborating at home as well as in the kitchen, the Hills have three sons. They value family time, and with both parents cooking every night, the boys often spend time at the restaurant. Two already work with their parents in the kitchen. The third son? "We're waiting until he can reach the sink," Jan says.

PAN-SEARED SCALLOPS SERVED OVER PESTO PASTA

(SERVES 2)

For the pesto:

2 cups fresh basil leaves
1 cup fresh baby spinach leaves
6 cloves garlic, peeled
Sea salt
½ cup olive oil
¼ cup almonds
¾ cup grated Parmesan cheese

For the pasta:

Salt
½ pound dry Italian linguine

For the scallops:

2 tablespoons melted clarified butter
10 (U-10) dry (diver) scallops
Hawaiian black lava salt

To make the pesto: Rinse and spin-dry basil and spinach leaves. Place basil, spinach, garlic, sea salt to taste, olive oil, and almonds in a food processor. Pulse until well blended. Add Parmesan cheese and pulse quickly just to blend cheese into pesto. Set aside.

To prepare the pasta: Bring a pot of salted water to a boil over medium-high heat. Add linguine and cook to al dente following package instructions. Drain in a colander.

To prepare the scallops: While pasta is cooking, place a large nonstick sauté pan over high heat. When pan is hot, add clarified butter. Place scallops in the pan, allowing space around each. Sear scallops on each side for about

2–3 minutes, until scallops have a caramelized glaze and have just cooked through and become opaque at the center.

To assemble: During the last minute the scallops are cooking, place hot linguine in a large bowl. Add about ¼ cup pesto and toss well with tongs. Divide linguine between 2 individual pasta bowls. Place 5 scallops atop each portion of pasta (4 in a square and 1 on top as a tower). Drizzle scallops with remaining pan butter. Sprinkle with black lava salt. Serve immediately.

Voodoo Seafood Stew

(SERVES 2 HEARTY PORTIONS)

1 cup fish stock

1 ounce eel sauce

½ cup white wine

3 cloves garlic, chopped

Pinch of saffron

Hot sauce (heat level 6)

8 ounces black grouper, cut into 1-inch cubes

6 ounces shrimp, peeled and deveined

4 ounces calamari, cut into rings with tentacles

Seafood seasoning of choice

Salt and freshly ground black pepper

4 ounces broccoli florets

2 shallots, sliced

1 red bell pepper, sliced

1 cup large-dice tomatoes

Place fish stock, eel sauce, wine, garlic, saffron, and hot sauce, to taste, in a medium pot over high heat. Season grouper, shrimp, and calamari with seafood seasoning, salt, and pepper to taste. Add seafood to pot, distributing it evenly in the stock mixture. Bring to a simmer, cover, and cook until seafood is almost opaque, about 2–3 minutes.

Distribute the vegetables evenly over the top of the stew. Re-cover and cook for an additional 2–3 minutes, just until seafood is cooked through and vegetables are crisp-tender.

Divide stew with broth between 2 large bowls and serve immediately.

Keys Fisheries Market & Marina

3502 Louisa Street (turn left on 37th Street)
Marathon, FL 33050
keysfisheries.com
(866) 743-4353
Gary Graves, Vice President

"John Travolta, your meal is up!" announces Keys Fisheries' restaurant server Penny over the loudspeaker. She grins as she watches first-time customers lined up at the order window furtively look around for a glimpse of the actor. By the time Meryl Streep, Robert Redford, and Marlon Brando are summoned, everyone gets the picture: Choose the name of your favorite actor as your order pickup moniker.

"We try to make eating fun, and we try to laugh a bit, too," says Gary Graves, vice president of Keys Fisheries, when speaking of the restaurant adjoining the commercial fishing operation of the same name. They take this humor mantra seriously. The order window theme is different every day. The bar name changes once a year, the result of a staff vote on customer suggestions. And, the winner of the annual stone-crab-eating contest is awarded a Caribbean cruise. (The money raised from admission to these events goes to local charities.)

This is an order-and-pick-up-the-food-yourself, paper-plates-and-plastic, sit-at-picnic-tables-on-the-dock-overlooking-Florida-Bay, pure Keys type of place. The fish and seafood couldn't be fresher, traveling about 100 feet from boat to kitchen.

Owned by Joe's Stone Crabs since 1967, the commercial fishery was originally established to supply stone crabs to the Miami restaurant. Graves has been with Keys Fisheries since the beginning, coming to the Keys from Wisconsin at age twenty-one. "I guess if you find something you like, you can stick with it," he says.

The fishing captains own their own boats, but Keys Fisheries supplies the land to store their traps and a place to dock their boats, and the fishery purchases everything the captains bring in. Stone crabs and Florida lobsters are the main

business here; finfish are caught solely for restaurant and fish market use. Most stone crabs are sent to Joe's; most lobsters are exported, mainly to China.

Making sauces, soups, and key lime pies in-house, Keys Fisheries' restaurant has become a bit of a test kitchen. The items became so popular, the fishery now wholesales them, supplying Whole Foods, Ocean Reef, and Sysco, among others. "It started out as a means to keep employees on staff when there were no lobsters or stone crabs available, but now we have a full production staff," says Graves. Their latest invention: konchwurst, a sausage-type link stuffed with ground conch.

And, the signature sandwich? Lobster Reuben . . . more than 200,000 sold and still counting!

Sautéed Lobster Tails

(SERVES 2)

4 tablespoons clarified butter

¼ cup flour

2 (6–8 ounce) Florida lobster tails, split in half

½ cup chopped scallions

Salt and freshly ground black pepper

1 teaspoon chopped (medium-fine) garlic

1 teaspoon chopped (medium-fine) shallots

3 ounces white wine

1 ounce fresh lemon juice

1 tablespoon flour

1 tablespoon whole butter

2 lemon wedges

2 sprigs parsley

Heat clarified butter in a large sauté pan over high heat. Lightly flour the meat side of tails and place them in the pan, meat-side down. Cook until lightly browned (about 3 minutes for 6-ounce tails). Turn tails, meat-side up, and add scallions and salt and pepper to taste. Cook an additional 2 minutes.

Remove tails from pan and add garlic, shallots, wine, and lemon juice to the pan. Whisk to combine. Sprinkle flour into wine mixture and whisk until thickened slightly. Stir in whole butter until melted. Remove from heat and whisk sauce.

Place 2 cooked half-tails on each of 2 dinner plates, shell-side down. Drizzle sauce over lobster. Garnish each portion with a lemon wedge and a sprig of parsley. Serve immediately.

Castaway Waterfront Restaurant & Sushi Bar

1406 Oceanview Avenue, MM-48, Oceanside
Marathon, FL 33050
(305) 743-6247
jonesn4sushi.com
John and Arlene Mirabella, Owners

"I had a Tom Sawyer upbringing," states John Mirabella. "I grew up living on a sailboat in Titusville, Florida. My father wanted to cast off every Friday afternoon after my mother got off work. When we heard her high heels clicking down the aluminum dock, my dad would yell, 'Cut the lines loose!' Then we'd sail away for the weekend."

John and wife Arlene also cast off and sailed away, commandeering their sailboat from Los Angeles to the Keys, a journey of ten and a half sailing weeks that spanned two years of vacation time. With a backstory like that, is it any wonder that John would finally choose to throw away his corporate tie in 1999 and buy a rundown 1950s restaurant in Marathon named Castaway?

"We had no experience in the restaurant business," says John, "but we had traveled a lot and we love to cook." Good thing, because the restaurant came with a dishwasher, but no chef. The Mirabellas donned aprons and kept things simple. "We had twelve menu items," says John. "Steamed shrimp—seconds on the house—and fresh honey buns were the most popular."

The Mirabellas had a couple of hiccups transforming the old Castaway (basically a screened-in porch that seated forty) into the popular seafood eatery it is today (an expansive glassed-in dining room boasting the largest menu in Marathon). In 2005

Hurricane Wilma flooded the restaurant, and the entire dining room floor collapsed eighteen months later. John and Arlene took it all in stride, re-creating the space into a welcoming gathering spot.

Though John and Arlene, who was born in the Philippines, have no formal culinary training, they use their considerable innate talents to develop their far-ranging menu selections, adding a sushi bar in 2004. "I like unique food," John says. For the Beef Yu-Ke, for instance, he likes to break the quail egg yolk over the beef before he begins eating. "I call it Mother Nature's gravy," he says.

John Mirabella spearfishes nearly every day, providing at least half the fresh fish that makes it to his dining tables. This catch includes lionfish, the invasive predator that is decimating the small fish on the coral reef (see sidebar on page 78).

Tucked away on a canal, down a series of winding residential lanes, Castaway Waterfront Restaurant & Sushi Bar is easy to miss. But locals will tell you, "It's worth the search."

Castaway's Wreck Diver-Style Lionfish

(SERVES 6)

2 cups flour

Old Bay Seasoning

6 (7-ounce) lionfish fillets*, rinsed and patted dry with
    paper towels

3 tablespoons butter

5 cloves garlic, chopped

2½ cups chopped tomatoes

5 teaspoons capers, drained

½ cup white wine

¼ cup fresh-squeezed lemon juice

2 tablespoons chopped fresh basil

6 sprigs parsley

6 lemon wedges

To prepare the lionfish: Place flour on a dinner plate and season with Old Bay to taste. Dredge fillets in flour to lightly dust.

Place butter in a large sauté pan over medium heat. (Melted butter should cover the bottom of the pan; add more if necessary.) When butter has melted, add fillets. Cook until undersides are golden, about 2–3 minutes. (Take care that they don't burn.) Gently turn fillets over. Reduce heat to low.

Mix garlic, tomatoes, capers, wine, and lemon juice in a medium bowl. Pour mixture over fish. Cover and cook until the fish flakes when tested gently with a fork. Sprinkle with basil.

To plate and serve: Place a fillet on each of 6 dinner plates. Spoon sauce atop fillets. Garnish with a sprig of parsley and a lemon wedge. Serve immediately.

*If you can't find 7-ounce fillets, substitute an equivalent amount of smaller fillets and adjust the cooking time accordingly. And if you don't have lionfish, substitute other sweet white-fleshed fish fillets.

Beef Yu-Ke (Asian Raw Beef Salad)

(SERVES 2 AS AN APPETIZER)

8 ounces high-quality center-cut sirloin
¼ cup sesame oil
¼ cup kimchi base
2 iceberg lettuce leaves or 1 large kale leaf
   divided into 2 pieces
1 tablespoon white sesame seeds
1 tablespoon black sesame seeds
4 scallions, sliced thin
2 quail eggs

Using a very sharp knife, carefully cut beef into a small dice that slightly resembles ground beef but is not as mushy. (There is a fine line between pieces being too big to chew and having a mushy texture. Sirloin is more forgiving. More tender cuts of meat quickly lose their texture.)

Place diced meat into a medium mixing bowl. Add sesame oil and kimchi base and toss to combine. (Kimchi is a personal taste, so add it sparingly to taste. Don't allow mixture to get too soupy.)

Place lettuce or kale leaf on each of 2 plates. Divide the beef equally and place on top of the greens. Mix the sesame seeds together in a small bowl. Sprinkle sesame seeds and scallions atop beef. Crack each quail egg over the sink and separate out the yolk. Place a yolk atop each portion of beef. Place Yu-Ke in refrigerator for 5 minutes to chill. Serve with chopsticks.

Bold and arrogant, lionfish sit among the coral crevasses awaiting the passing schools of fish fry, their unsuspecting prey. Their tropical beauty belies the lurking danger, a venomous gland at the base of every feathery quill, which they use to sting and stun their victims before gulping them en masse.

A relative of the parrotfish and native to the Indian Ocean, where they have a natural predator that eats their larvae, lionfish were dumped from tropical fish tanks into the waters of the Florida Keys, it is believed, where they quickly multiplied. With no predator in these waters and dropping 30,000 eggs every three to nine days, the fish reproduce unchecked.

The good news, however, is that on the table, lionfish is a moist, buttery delicacy, similar in taste and texture to hogfish, and lends itself to a wide variety of preparations. The bad news: Lionfish are not fished commercially. Because they cannot be caught with bait and line, they must be speared or be snagged as an incidental bycatch in lobster traps, and they are tricky to clean and fillet without injury. (Castaway Waterfront Restaurant in Marathon and Key Largo Conch House and the Fish House in Key Largo regularly serve lionfish. See profiles in this book.)

Experts believe that the Florida Keys cannot eradicate the species but can only work toward population control at best. To that end, dive masters hunt the lionfish, conservation organizations like REEF (Reef Environmental Education Foundation) host lionfish derbies, and fishermen haul them up by the hundreds from their lobster traps. Our job? Eat 'em!

No Name Pub

30813 N. Watson Boulevard, MM-31, Bayside
Big Pine Key, FL 33043
(305) 872-9115
NONAMEPUB.COM
Douglas Leps, General Manager

Perhaps the most colorful roadhouse in the Keys, No Name Pub—in one incarnation or another—has been operating since the early 1930s. Tucked at the foot of No Name Key Bridge in an out-of-the-way residential neighborhood on Big Pine Key, No Name sparkles as one of the Keys' hidden gems.

Pizza is the star attraction here, but the pub's decor and storied history steal the show. Once a general store/bait-and-tackle shop/eatery that also offered "ladies of the evening" upstairs, No Name Pub morphed, by the 1950s, into a beer-drinking, pool-shooting, dice-throwing, card-playing hangout that also served food.

Legend has it that in the late 1970s, a customer with a crush on the bartender was too shy to approach her, so he wrote his name and phone number on a dollar bill and left it on the bar on his way out. The bartender tacked the bill on the bulletin board. From then on, if she left the bar for a moment, she'd often find another signed dollar on the board when she returned. Thirty-five years later, the dark, intimate pub is literally wallpapered (inches thick) with dollar bills, signed and stapled onto the walls and ceiling by customers over the decades. The net worth of those walls? About $100,000!

No Name's famous pizza appeared in the 1960s, when two cooks from Italy bought the pub, bringing with them their old-world recipe, which they later wrote on the kitchen wall. No Name has been using this exact recipe for more than fifty years.

"We have a unique style of pizza," says Doug Leps, general manager of No Name Pub. "We call it 'inside-out' pizza." He explains that most pizzas are layered with sauce, cheese, and then toppings. No Name's pizza layers the sauce first, then all the toppings (except the pepperoni), then the cheese, and finally the pepperoni. This way, he says, "it steams the veggies under the cheese," rather than them drying out on top of the cheese. "It creates a different effect, a different taste."

The secret to No Name's great pizza, says Leps, is fourfold. The dough is made fresh every day and proofed for twelve to twenty-four hours. All the vegetables are chopped fresh every day. No compromise is ever made on the cheese—it is always "whole milk, 3 percent, mozzarella." And, finally, the pizza is cooked in a 650°F brick oven, which makes the bottom crispy but doesn't burn the top.

"We have a cult following," says Leps. "We don't advertise. People find us by word of mouth. Our customers come year after year, and they don't want anything to change." As the sign says: "No Name Pub, a nice place if you can find it."

ROYAL PUB PIZZA

(SERVES 3–4)

For the dough:

¾ cup cold water
¾ teaspoon olive oil
¾ teaspoon sugar
⅛ teaspoon salt
1½–2 cups high-gluten flour*
⅛ teaspoon instant yeast
2 tablespoons all-purpose flour
½ teaspoon cornmeal

For the sauce:

1 tablespoon olive oil
1 cup diced tomatoes
1 tablespoon minced garlic
1 teaspoon chopped fresh oregano
1 teaspoon chopped fresh basil
1 teaspoon dry Italian seasoning
1 cup tomato sauce
½ cup tomato paste

For the toppings:

½ cup diced, cooked Italian sausage
½ cup chopped fresh mushrooms
½ cup thinly sliced Spanish yellow onions
½ cup thinly sliced green bell peppers
¼ cup sliced black olives
1–1¼ cups shredded whole-milk mozzarella cheese
½ cup thinly sliced pepperoni

To make the dough: Place water, olive oil, sugar, and salt in the large bowl of an electric mixer. Mix on low speed for 3 minutes, until the sugar and salt are dissolved. Slowly add 1½ cups high-gluten flour and mix on low speed for 3 minutes. Add yeast and mix on medium speed for another 4 minutes. (Use additional flour if necessary to achieve proper dough consistency: dough forms a ball and comes away from the edges of the bowl.) Remove dough from bowl, forming it into a ball. Cover dough ball with plastic wrap and place in refrigerator. Allow dough to proof for at least 1 hour.

To make the sauce: Place olive oil in a large sauté pan over medium heat. Add tomatoes, garlic, oregano, basil, and Italian seasoning. Cook on medium-high for about 5 minutes, stirring often and pressing down on tomatoes with the spoon. Reduce heat to medium-low and simmer for another 10 minutes, stirring occasionally. Remove from heat. Stir in tomato sauce and tomato paste. Allow sauce to cool.

To make the pizza: Preheat oven to 450–500°F. Remove dough ball from refrigerator. Allow it to rest at room temperature for 5 minutes. Sprinkle the outside of the dough ball with 2 tablespoons all-purpose flour and roll it out to flatten the dough slightly. Pick up the dough from underneath, and using clean hands clenched into fists, stretch and spin the dough until you have a 14-inch round.

Dust a pizza pan or pizza stone with cornmeal and place stretched dough on it. Evenly spread ½ cup of sauce on the dough, leaving a 1-inch border around the outer edge. Evenly place sausage, mushrooms, onions, bell peppers, and black

olives atop the pizza. Sprinkle with mozzarella cheese. Place pepperoni slices atop cheese.

Bake pizza for 15–20 minutes or until the cheese begins to brown and crust is crisp. (You may have to bake pizza longer; No Name Pub uses a 650°F pizza oven.) Cut into 8 slices with a pizza cutter and serve immediately.

*High-gluten flour is different than all-purpose flour. High gluten gives the dough elasticity. In the supermarket, look for bakers' flour or bread flour.

Spicy Pub Conch Fritters

(MAKES 24 FRITTERS)

1½ cups Drake's Crispy Fry Mix* (or similar fry mix)

½ cup water

1 large egg, beaten

1 teaspoon granulated sugar

1 cup cleaned and chopped conch (no black pieces)

1 tablespoon chopped jalapeños

¼ cup finely diced red onions

¼ cup finely diced celery

⅛ cup finely diced red bell pepper

⅛ cup finely diced yellow bell pepper

⅛ cup finely diced green bell pepper

1 tablespoon minced garlic

Salt and freshly ground black pepper

Canola oil for frying

2 lemons, cut in wedges

1 cup cocktail sauce

½ cup honey mustard

Place fry mix, water, egg, and sugar in a medium bowl and stir until ingredients are well mixed and smooth. Add conch, jalapeños, onions, celery, bell peppers, garlic, and a pinch of salt and pepper. Stir until well mixed. (The consistency should be thick enough to hold a ball shape for a few seconds before falling apart. If necessary, add more fry mix to achieve proper consistency.) Cover mixture with plastic wrap and refrigerate for 30 minutes.

Heat oil in an electric deep-fat fryer to manufacturer's instructions. Remove conch mixture from refrigerator and, using two spoons, make 1-inch-round fritters (about ¾ ounce) and drop them into the hot oil. Cook fritters until they float and are a deep golden brown.

Remove fritters from oil with a slotted spoon and drain on paper towels. Place on a serving platter garnished with lemon wedges. Serve with small bowls of cocktail sauce and honey mustard for dipping.

*Drake's Crispy Fry Mix is available online.

Like most residents of the Florida Keys, key limes are not indigenous. Spanish conquistadors planted key lime seeds wherever they landed, including Haiti by 1520 and Mexico after the fall of the Aztec empire, so it is a safe bet they dropped a few in the Keys as well.

For centuries the tart juice of the yellow ping-pong-ball-size citrus (*Citrus aurantifolia* Swingle) has flavored nearly everything that has made it to the Keys table, from fish to fudge, soups to sauces, drinks to desserts. But nothing is more notable than the beloved key lime pie, dubbed the official dessert of the Florida Keys.

With the invention of sweetened condensed milk by Gail Borden in 1859, Keys cooks began making the quintessential citrus-custard pie filling, which was actually cooked by the high acidic content of the key lime juice. Although locals still debate if an authentic pie should have a pastry or graham cracker crust and be topped with whipped cream or meringue, history should hold the clues. Pie pastry was probably used in the nineteenth century, as graham crackers were undoubtedly not widely available in the Keys and, at any rate, would not have held up well in the heat and humidity in the days before refrigeration. And chances are, given the dearth of fresh milk products available in the Keys before 1912, whipped cream would have been an unlikely topping. When meringue began crowning the pie is anybody's guess.

In 2013 Key Westers David Sloan and Marky Pierson decided it was high time the tart elixir be honored with a festival of its own. Celebrated for three days in Key West over July Fourth weekend, the First Annual Key Lime Pie Festival

ranged from the sublime to the ridiculous. Professional and amateur bakers competed in a juried key lime pie championship—sublime. Ten brave eaters participated in the Mile High Key Lime Pie Eatin' Contest, where, outfitted with goggles and newspaper bibs and hands locked behind their backs, they raced to devour key lime pies topped with ten inches of whipped cream—hysterically ridiculous.

But the crowning feature of the entire festival was the assembly of a giant key lime pie by Sloan and Pierson along with Key West chefs Jim Brush and Paul Menta. Attempting to make the world's largest key lime pie, the men created their masterpiece.

Measuring 8 feet, 1 inch in diameter, 50.265 square feet in area, the pie served 909.31 hearty 7.96-inch-square slices! And what an ingredients list! It required 5,760 key limes, 55 gallons of sweetened condensed milk, 200 pounds of graham crackers, 41 pounds of brown sugar, 8 pounds of honey, 112 pounds of butter, three "top secret" ingredients, and, insists David Sloan, "2,369 gallons of Key West love." Now an annual event, the Key Lime Pie Festival continues to spread the love.

MANNY & ISA'S KEY LIME PIE

(SERVES 8)

This pie may not have broken any world records, but it reigns supreme in my book. Developed by Manny & Isa's Kitchen, which closed its doors about a decade ago, this is one of the best recipes for the traditional pastry piecrust and meringue-topping version of key lime pie that I have ever tasted. Manny gave me his recipe for the first edition of *Insiders' Guide to the Florida Keys and Key West,* which I wrote in 1995.

4 large or 6 medium eggs
1 (14-ounce) can Eagle Brand sweetened condensed milk
4 ounces key lime juice
1 prepared piecrust, baked and cooled
¼ teaspoon cream of tartar
½ cup sugar

Preheat oven to 375°F. Separate egg yolks from whites. Put whites aside for use in meringue. Place yolks in a medium bowl and beat with an electric mixer until frothy. Add sweetened condensed milk and mix together. Add key lime juice and mix again. Pour into baked, cooled piecrust.

Thoroughly wash and dry bowl and beaters. Place egg whites in a medium bowl. Beat with an electric mixer until medium peaks form. Add cream of tartar and continue to beat. Add sugar slowly and continue beating until mixture is stiff.

Spread meringue over pie, sealing it to the crust. Bake until meringue is golden brown, about 15 minutes. Refrigerate key lime pie until chilled.

THE DINING ROOM AT LITTLE PALM ISLAND

28500 OVERSEAS HIGHWAY, MM-28.5, OCEANSIDE
LITTLE TORCH KEY, FL 33042
(305) 872-2551
LITTLEPALMISLAND.COM
ROLANDO CRUZ-TAURA, EXECUTIVE CHEF

Without a doubt the most exclusive, romantic restaurant in the Florida Keys, the Dining Room at Little Palm Island stands alone among its peers. Situated on a five-acre island, three miles offshore Little Torch Key in the Atlantic Ocean, the focal point of the exquisite Noble House resort, Little Palm—as locals affectionately refer to the restaurant—offers an ambience as reminiscent of a South Seas island as one can get in the continental United States.

Diners board a launch from the island's substation on Little Torch Key for the short cruise to the island. With panoramic views of the palm-peppered beach and the moonbeam-shimmering ocean from virtually every facet of the restaurant, guests can choose to dine in the elegant, candlelit dining room, on the terrace perched above the beach, or at torch-lit tables sprinkled along the water's edge.

At first blush it might seem that creating a cuisine that can measure up to this amazing backdrop would be a Herculean feat. But executive chef Rolando "Roly" Cruz-Taura's significant culinary talents more than match the restaurant's astonishing environment.

Born and raised in Miami's "Little Havana" neighborhood, Cruz-Taura spent a lot of time in his Cuban grandmother's kitchen. He progressed from baking cookies to more complex dishes, even taking over his oldest brother's task of creating the Thanksgiving meal one year. Working in restaurant kitchens during his college years at Georgia Institute of Technology, Cruz-Taura discovered, "I was much happier in the hospitality industry than studying mechanical engineering."

Transferring to Florida International University, Cruz-Taura earned a degree in hospitality management and then embarked on a most impressive culinary journey, working under the tutelage of some of the most honored chefs in Miami. Hand-picked as his successor in 2012 by Little Palm's Luis Puis—the renowned executive chef who put Little Palm's cuisine on the map—Cruz-Taura pairs a vibrant blend of Pan-Latin ingredients with French techniques to create Little Palm's signature cuisine, which he dubs "modern tropical." "Chef Luis catapulted Little Palm Island into a new level of excellence," says Cruz-Taura. "I feel honored that he entrusted me to continue his vision."

"I love to eat as much as I love to create," he says of creating new dishes for Little Palm. "I sample dishes from all over the world when I travel. I read cookbooks like they were novels, seeing what other chefs are doing and how I can incorporate techniques, ingredients, and presentations." Cruz-Taura adds, "We change our entire dinner menu daily, repeating highly requested items only every few days. It's a challenge, but one that I look forward to every day."

"I always feel that as chefs we are merely caretakers of a restaurant and its cuisine," he states modestly. "We take on the responsibility of running the day-to-day and aspire to elevate the quality and creativity of what we offer until the reins are passed on to the next generation." Speaking of Little Palm Island, Cruz-Taura says, "We are in the business of creating memories that will last a lifetime."

Lobster with Roasted Corn & Apple Risotto

(SERVES 4)

For the lobster:

2 (1½-pound) steamed whole Maine lobsters
¼ cup extra-virgin olive oil
1 teaspoon fresh lime juice
Salt and freshly ground black pepper
1 bay leaf
1 stick unsalted butter

For the corn broth:

1 quart water
4 corncobs, kernels removed and reserved for risotto
Salt
1 bay leaf
3 sprigs fresh thyme

For the corn risotto:

1 cup reserved corn kernels
6 cups chicken broth
2 cups prepared corn broth
¼ cup extra-virgin olive oil
1 small yellow onion, finely diced
3 cloves garlic, minced
2 cups arborio rice
½ cup dry white wine
½ cup peeled and small-diced Granny Smith apple
½ cup mascarpone cheese
½ cup grated Parmesan cheese
2 tablespoons butter
1 tablespoon truffle oil
Salt and freshly ground black pepper

For the garnishes:

½ cup shaved (on a mandolin) fresh fennel bulb
1 teaspoon extra-virgin olive oil
Salt and freshly ground black pepper
2 tablespoons snipped fresh chives

To prepare the lobster: Remove lobster meat from the shells, leaving the claws whole and splitting the tails in half. Place the lobster meat in a large mixing bowl and drizzle with olive oil and lime juice. Season with salt and pepper to taste. Transfer lobster mixture to a shallow sauté pan. Add bay leaf, butter, and enough water to cover the lobsters. Set aside until needed.

To make the corn broth: Place water, corncobs, 1 tablespoon salt, bay leaf, and thyme in a large saucepan over medium heat and simmer until liquid has reduced by half. Pour through a fine-mesh strainer. Adjust salt to taste. Set broth aside until ready to use. Discard cobs.

To make the corn risotto: Place reserved corn kernels in a small sauté pan and dry-roast them over medium heat until they begin to char slightly. Remove from heat and set aside. Place chicken and corn broths in a large saucepan and bring to a simmer over medium heat.

Place olive oil in a separate large saucepan over medium-high heat. When oil is hot, add onions and garlic and sweat them until fragrant. Add rice to the pan and stir until all the kernels are coated with oil. Add wine and stir rice until wine evaporates. Add 1 cup of hot broth and continue stirring rice until broth has been absorbed. Repeat this process, adding 1 cup broth at a time.

When rice is cooked al dente, add roasted corn and apples. Stir to combine. Fold in mascarpone, Parmesan cheese, butter, and truffle oil. Season with salt and pepper to taste.

To plate and serve: Place sauté pan of lobster over low to medium heat and reheat until warmed through. Place shaved fennel and olive oil in a small bowl and toss to combine. Season with salt and pepper to taste.

Divide finished risotto into 4 serving bowls. Top each with a half lobster tail and 1 claw. Top each portion with an equal amount of shaved fennel and snipped chives. Serve immediately.

TEQUILA CEVICHE LITTLE PALM ISLAND

(SERVES 4 AS AN APPETIZER)

1 pound fresh wahoo, snapper, grouper, or
   mahi-mahi fillets

1 tablespoon kosher salt

¼ cup sugar

½ cup rice wine vinegar

2 teaspoons seeded and minced habanero chilies

Juice and zest from 8 tangerines

3 tablespoons silver tequila

1 tablespoon fresh lime juice

1 ripe avocado

1 tablespoon extra-virgin olive oil

1 tablespoon finely chopped fresh mint

2 tablespoons sliced scallions

Crispy plantain chips

Tortilla strips

To prepare the ceviche: Dice the fish into ¼-inch pieces. Place fish in a large bowl and toss with salt. Set aside for 20 minutes.

Meanwhile, place sugar and vinegar in a small saucepan over medium heat. Heat, stirring frequently, until sugar dissolves. Remove saucepan from heat. Add chilies, tangerine juice and zest, tequila, and lime juice to the vinegar/sugar mixture. Whisk to combine.

Pour dressing over fish and toss to combine. Cover bowl with plastic wrap and refrigerate for at least 1 hour but no more than 3 hours. Stir mixture occasionally.

To serve: Peel and seed avocado and cut into small dice. Stir oil and mint into fish mixture. Divide ceviche among 4 bowls or plates. Top each portion with ½ tablespoon sliced scallions and one-quarter of the diced avocado. Stick a few crispy plantain chips and tortilla strips into the ceviche. Serve the rest of the chips and strips in a basket on the side.

SQUARE GROUPER BAR & GRILL

22658 OVERSEAS HIGHWAY, MM-22.5, OCEANSIDE
CUDJOE KEY, FL 33042
(305) 745-8880
SQUAREGROUPERBARANDGRILL.COM
LYNN BELL, CHEF AND OWNER

"I kind of grew up around square grouper during my high school years," says Lynn Bell, explaining the story behind the theme of her popular restaurant. "Our family would vacation in Marathon a lot in the 1970s, when marijuana smuggling was very prevalent. You could almost walk across the bay on square grouper some days," she recounts.

For those not familiar with Bell's inspiration, "square grouper" was the nickname given square packages of weed dropped in the ocean waters off the Florida Keys by drug smugglers and then fished out by their land-based business partners. When the packages got tangled in fishermen's lines, they dubbed the catch "square grouper."

Lithe and serene, Bell exudes warmth, individuality, and a certain quirkiness that explains the tongue-in-cheek references to the smuggled cannabis in everything from logos to decor. Tables, plates, poof seats, and T-shirt cubbies are all square. The floor tile is imprinted with green grass, the thresholds with smoke, as in "smoke grass." The restaurant smokes its own fish and pork, so "This joint is smokin'!" joins "Smoked, baked, and fried!" and "My favorite joint!" as logos for the restaurant.

Bell's creativity is apparent in Square Grouper's cuisine as well. A self-taught chef whose only professional culinary credential was cooking three meals a day each summer for the staff of her parents' Vermont inn during her teenage years, Bell dove in head first, opening Square Grouper in 2003. "I knew nothing about the business aspect," she says, "but I had tablets of food concepts" concocted over the years. Bell creates all the menus, recipes, and specials, but she credits her "awesome staff" for the restaurant's success: "We get along great," she says.

Utilizing the Keys' fresh fish and seafood, Bell describes her restaurant's cuisine as New American with ethnic influences. Jasmine rice bowls and innovative pastas join

the piscatorial offerings on the menu. "I try to keep it vibrant," she says. "I get crazy ideas and then adapt them to work for our kitchen." In 2014 Bell expanded Square Grouper, adding an upstairs cocktail/tapas lounge named My New Joint, whose "wink-wink" logo reads: "Because two joints are better than one!"

The karma of Square Grouper is the most important thing to Bell. "When people walk through the front door, they say they feel happy," she says. "I have two mottos," she continues, "'A clean kitchen is a happy kitchen' and 'Enjoy what you do and you'll never work a day in your life.'" And with characteristic wry humor she adds, "I got that last one out of a *Playboy* magazine, actually!"

Toasted Almond-Encrusted Grouper with Warm Caribbean Pineapple Relish

(SERVES 4)

For the sweet potatoes:

4 sweet potatoes
½ cup butter
2 teaspoons salt
2 teaspoons black pepper
1 tablespoon cider vinegar
½ cup Vermont maple syrup

For the pineapple relish:

1 cup butter
1 cup light brown sugar
2 teaspoons Jamaican jerk seasoning
½ cup sun-dried cranberries
1 fresh ripe pineapple, peeled and cut into uniform bite-size squares

For the grouper:

1 cup sliced almonds, divided
2 cups panko crumbs
⅓ cup chopped fresh flat-leaf parsley
4 (9-ounce) fillets fresh local black grouper (or other flakey, white-fleshed fish)
Salt and freshly ground black pepper
¼ cup canola oil
4 lemon wedges

To prepare the sweet potatoes: Preheat oven to 350°F. Bake potatoes for 50 minutes or until soft. Peel off skins and place potatoes in a large bowl. Add butter, salt, pepper, vinegar, and syrup and mash until smooth.

To make the pineapple relish: Place butter in a medium saucepan over medium-low heat. Add brown sugar and whisk until sugar has dissolved and mixture is smooth. Add jerk seasoning, cranberries, and pineapple and simmer for 20 minutes. Reduce heat to low, cover, and keep sauce warm until needed.

To prepare the grouper: Preheat oven to 400°F. Spread ½ cup sliced almonds on a baking sheet and place in oven for 5 minutes, until almonds are golden brown. (Watch carefully so they don't burn.) Remove almonds from oven and set aside.

Mix panko crumbs, remaining ½ cup almonds, and parsley in a medium bowl. Place crumb mixture on a dinner plate. Season the grouper fillets with salt and pepper. Press fillets into the panko mixture until well coated on both sides.

Heat canola oil in a large nonstick skillet over medium heat. Add grouper fillets and sauté for 3 minutes per side (depending upon thickness) until cooked through.

To assemble: Mound one-quarter of the mashed sweet potatoes in the center of each dinner plate. Place a sautéed grouper fillet atop each sweet potato mound. Top each with ½ cup warm pineapple relish and sprinkle with toasted almonds. Garnish each serving with a lemon wedge.

Island Shrimp Cakes with Island Pepper Aioli

(SERVES 4)

For the aioli:

2 cups mayonnaise

¼ cup minced banana peppers

⅛ cup minced pickled jalapeños

1 tablespoon key lime juice

1 tablespoon minced garlic

Salt and freshly ground black pepper

For the shrimp cakes:

2 pounds cooked, peeled, and deveined
    shrimp (16/20s)

½ cup chopped red onions

½ cup chopped red bell peppers

½ cup minced banana peppers

⅛ cup minced jalapeños

Zest from 1 lemon

2 eggs, beaten

¾ cup fresh lemon juice

¾ cup mayonnaise

1 teaspoon Tabasco sauce

2 teaspoons Old Bay Seasoning

2 cups panko crumbs

4 tablespoons canola oil, divided

For the garnishes:

12 sprigs dill, chives, or parsley

2 lemons, each cut into 6 wedges

To make the aioli: Place mayonnaise, banana peppers, jalapeños, key lime juice, and garlic in a medium bowl and stir to mix well. Season with salt and pepper to taste. Transfer to a covered container and refrigerate until needed.

To prepare shrimp cakes: Preheat oven to 425°F. Chop shrimp into small, bite-size pieces and transfer to a large bowl. Add onions, bell and banana peppers, jalapeños, lemon zest, eggs, lemon juice, mayonnaise, Tabasco, and Old Bay and mix well. Add panko crumbs to bind ingredients together. (You do not have to use all 2 cups.)

Form shrimp mixture into twelve 2-inch cakes. Place 2 tablespoons canola oil in a large nonstick skillet over high heat. Add 6 shrimp cakes and sear each side until golden brown. Transfer to a baking sheet. Add remaining 2 tablespoons oil to skillet and repeat searing process with remaining 6 shrimp cakes. Transfer to baking sheet. Place shrimp cakes in oven and bake for 10 minutes.

To serve: Place 3 shrimp cakes on each plate. Place a button of aioli (about the size of a nickel) atop each shrimp cake. Garnish with an herb sprig and a lemon wedge.

Kaya Island Eats

3100 Overseas Highway, MM-14.5, Oceanside
Saddlebunch Keys, FL 33042
(305) 328-8303
KAYAISLANDEATS.COM
Scott Taylor, Chef and Owner

Scott Taylor rides his passions like the waves of his surfer-dude youth growing up on the Hawaiian island of Maui. Nowhere does his passion shine as brightly as at Kaya Island Eats, his restaurant dream that became a reality in 2011, with the help of his partner, Gabriela Espinoza, whom he calls "the love of my life!" Together they have created an island oasis with a "touch of aloha" apparent in everything from the eclectic cuisine, to the sparkling water vistas from every window, to the caring welcome they extend to their guests.

"I am a culinary school dropout," states Taylor. "It interfered with my surfing." Preferring the kitchen to the classroom, Taylor went right to work in a commercial kitchen, learning his craft. "Nothing can be traded for a row of tickets, the sweaty environment, music blaring, food going out of the kitchen," he expounds. "It is a beautiful symphony of sound and smell."

After years of cooking in such Hawaiian restaurants as the Ritz-Carlton Kapalua, Taylor found himself at the end of a marriage and in need of a change. "My parents were Parrot Heads," says Taylor, referring to the loyal fans of singer Jimmy Buffett. "They had a house in Key West and urged me to use it to decompress. After a three-month party sabbatical, I decided it was time for a job!"

Taylor managed the popular Key West restaurant Blue Heaven for nearly ten years before opening Kaya Island Eats. "Items on my menu are things I've been dreaming up since my teenage years," he says. "I put my heart and soul into my food." Most chefs learn French techniques of cooking, but for Taylor in Hawaii, techniques he encountered were basically Asian. "Hawaiian food isn't Hawaiian anymore," he says. "Like the people who live there, it is a melting pot of flavors and cultures."

And that is what he brings to his cuisine at Kaya, which he describes as "New Island" or "Jawaiian"—the fusion of Jamaican, Asian, South Pacific, Indian, and Caribbean cuisines. "I have found a sweet balance between being unique and being true to my vision, which is doing dishes that are different but accessible," he explains.

"Kaya named itself," Taylor states. "In my head, my dream restaurant was always Kaya." He goes on to explain: "Every culture has a different meaning for 'kaya.' For me, Kaya is a Bob Marley song. Kaya is a coconut jam from Malaysia that I loved as a kid. Kaya is the ultimate state of mind—that feeling you have when you're completely in the groove. Imagine taking off your shoes and dancing in the sand. That's what Kaya means to me!"

Pacific Rim Tuna Poke

(SERVES 4)

For the marinade/sauce:

1 tablespoon black sesame seeds
1 tablespoon white sesame seeds
2 scallions, thinly sliced
1½ cups soy sauce
2 tablespoons sesame oil
1 tablespoon grated fresh gingerroot
1 tablespoon minced pickled jalapeños
2 tablespoons toasted, finely chopped
    macadamia nuts

For the wasabi aioli:

½ cup mayonnaise
3–4 cloves garlic, chopped
2–3 tablespoons wasabi powder

For the tuna poke and to serve:

2 pounds sashimi-grade yellowfin tuna
Wonton chips or rice crackers
2 ounces seaweed salad (wakame), optional
1 teaspoon flying fish roe (Tobiko caviar), optional

To make the marinade/sauce: Preheat oven to 325°F. Place sesame seeds on a baking sheet and toast lightly in oven until white seeds turn tan. Place scallions, soy sauce, sesame oil, gingerroot, jalapeños, and macadamia nuts in a food processor. Pulse until well blended. Add toasted sesame seeds to marinade. Pulse once to blend. Transfer marinade to a covered container and refrigerate for 20 minutes to allow flavors to marry.

To make the wasabi aioli: Place mayonnaise, garlic, and wasabi powder in a blender. Blend on low speed until mixture is smooth. (Use lesser amount of wasabi powder for a milder aioli, greater amount for a more spicy aioli.) Transfer to a covered container and refrigerate until needed.

To prepare the tuna poke: Cut tuna into ¼-inch cubes. Place tuna and marinade in a medium bowl and stir to combine. Cover bowl and refrigerate tuna for at least 10 minutes or up to

1 hour, so that tuna and marinade flavors can marry. (If tuna marinates for more than 1 hour, it will become too salty.)

To serve: Remove tuna from marinade with a slotted spoon. Place a small amount of tuna poke on each wonton chip or rice cracker. Drizzle with aioli. Top each with a garnish of seaweed salad and a sprinkling of caviar if desired. Place 4 or 5 poke-topped wontons on each of 4 appetizer plates and serve immediately.

Rasta Pasta with Macadamia Nut Jerk Pesto

(SERVES 4)

For the pesto:

6 cloves garlic, peeled

⅛ cup macadamia nuts

¼ cup Parmesan cheese

2 teaspoons kosher salt

2 teaspoons black pepper

2 tablespoons Caribbean jerk seasoning

2 cups (8 ounces) fresh basil, leaves and crowns only, stems discarded

½ cup first-cold-pressed olive oil

⅛ cup extra-virgin hemp oil or first-cold-pressed olive oil

For the pasta:

1 (12-ounce) box angel hair pasta (for gluten-free, use pad thai rice noodles)

1 tablespoon olive oil

4 tablespoons freshly grated Parmesan cheese, divided

½ cup chopped fresh tomato, divided

4 fresh basil crowns

To make the pesto: Place garlic in a food processor and pulse until finely chopped. Add nuts, cheese, salt, and pepper and process until finely chopped. Add jerk seasoning and basil and pulse until finely chopped. With processor running, slowly add both oils until the pesto becomes a thick paste. Transfer to a covered container and refrigerate pesto until needed.

To prepare the pasta: Bring a large pot of water to a boil over high heat. Add pasta and cook to al dente following package instructions. (If using rice noodles, be very careful not to overcook them.) Drain cooked pasta.

Place a large sauté pan over medium heat and add 1 tablespoon olive oil. When oil is warm, add pesto and cook, stirring constantly, until pesto has reached that "magical place" between warm and hot. Stir angel hair into pesto and divide pasta among 4 individual pasta bowls. Sprinkle each serving with 1 tablespoon Parmesan cheese, 2 tablespoons chopped tomato, and a basil crown. Serve immediately.

KEY WEST

Arranged alphabetically

Azur Restaurant

425 Grinnell Street
Key West, FL 33040
(305) 292-2987
AZURKEYWEST.COM
Michael Mosi, Chef and Owner
Drew Wenzel, Chef and Owner

Friends since 1986, when they met in the Allen Room kitchen, working their way through Penn State University, Drew Wenzel and Michael Mosi bounce their sentences off each other like ping-pong balls. "We couldn't stand each other for the first three days," recounts Wenzel. "Then we realized we had the same goals but two completely different paths of getting there," Mosi interjects.

After graduation the two headed in different directions. Wenzel moved to Germany and studied culinary arts as a journeyman, becoming a certified chef. Mosi went straight to work in a series of restaurant kitchens throughout the United States. Friendship and serendipity kept the friends connected in the ensuing years. When Wenzel opened Graceland, his authentic American Southern cuisine restaurant in Hamburg, he called on Mosi to join him. Years later, after Mosi trotted the globe, living and working in Italy, Greece, Thailand, and South Africa, he landed in Key West as executive chef at Antonia's. Mosi asked Wenzel to cook by his side.

The friends opened Azur in 2007. "Azur is the restaurant we always talked about having," says Wenzel. "We wanted to highlight the seafood of this town," adds Mosi. The cuisine was to be coastal Mediterranean, and they wanted the restaurant's name to reflect that. Mosi recalled, "We literally floated in the pool with tumblers of vodka to get

our creative juices flowing." The sun and blue water conjured up the Côte de Azur. Voila, Azur it was! "We do feed off each other that way," says Wenzel. Mosi jokingly adds, "We definitely can inspire each other to great torment and great brilliance!"

According to Mosi, "Everything we do now is based on history. We plunged ourselves into cultures around the world to understand why the dishes were there, what was available locally, and what the history behind the food was." Wenzel adds, "Culture, language, and cuisine are the same. Unless you've lived it, you can't understand it."

Their philosophy and experience is evident in their imaginative cuisine. Describing themselves as ingredient-driven chefs, they like to utilize every ounce and facet of an ingredient. "One of us is always here," says Wenzel, who handles breakfast and lunch, to Mosi's dinner service. "That's why we have such staying power."

"It's just like when we were in college. The rapport is still there, the way we come up with stuff," says Wenzel. "You know what it's going to be like," finishes Mosi with a laugh. "We're going to be those two eighty-year-old guys feeding the pigeons in the park, and the grandchildren will say, 'Not that story again. I don't want to hear it!'"

CARAMELIZED BRUSSELS SPROUTS
WITH PANCETTA & PECORINO ROMANO
(SERVES 4 AS A SIDE DISH)

1 pound brussels sprouts
2 tablespoons olive oil
4 ounces pancetta, cubed
1 shallot, minced
2 tablespoons Dijon mustard
2 tablespoons sugar
2 tablespoons sherry vinegar
Small piece of aged Pecorino Romano cheese

Preheat oven to 400°F. Bring a pot of water to a boil over high heat. Add brussels sprouts and blanch them for 5 minutes. Drain brussels sprouts.

Heat olive oil in a large sauté pan over medium-high heat. Add pancetta and sauté until crispy. Remove with a slotted spoon and place on a small plate. Add shallots and sauté until translucent. Stir in mustard, sugar, and sherry vinegar. Return pancetta to the pan and stir in brussels sprouts, coating them in the shallot dressing.

Transfer brussels sprouts mixture to a baking dish and bake until sprouts are caramelized, about 20 minutes. Sprinkle with Pecorino Romano cheese and serve immediately.

ROESTI BENEDICT

(SERVES 4)

For the potato pancakes:

2 large Yukon gold potatoes, peeled and
    coarsely grated
¾ cup (about 3 ounces) grated Parmesan cheese
Salt and freshly ground black pepper
Canola oil for frying

For the hollandaise sauce:

3 egg yolks
Juice of ½ lemon
2 tablespoons white wine
3 tablespoons hot water
2 sticks butter, melted
Salt

For the poached eggs:

1 quart water
2 tablespoons white vinegar
4 large eggs

For assembly:

4 (1-ounce) slices Brie cheese
4 thin slices prosciutto de Parma, trimmed slightly
    smaller than the pancake in size
Handful of arugula leaves

To make the potato pancakes: Preheat oven to 200°F. Mix grated potatoes and Parmesan cheese and season with salt and pepper to taste. Form potato mixture into four 4-inch pancakes. Pour enough oil in a large sauté pan to cover the bottom and place over medium-high heat. When oil is hot, add potato pancakes and fry until edges are golden brown, about 3 minutes per side. Remove pancakes to a heatproof plate and place them in the oven to keep warm.

To make the hollandaise sauce: In a double boiler over a water bath, whisk egg yolks, lemon juice, wine, and water, cooking until mixture is frothy, about 2 minutes. Slowly whisk in the melted butter and season with salt to taste. Remove from heat and use immediately.

To prepare the poached eggs: Meanwhile, place water and vinegar in a medium saucepan over medium heat and bring to a simmer (not a boil). Stir water once with a wooden spoon. Crack eggs into the center of the simmering water, one at a time, and cook for 2 minutes. Remove poached eggs with a slotted spoon and serve immediately.

To assemble the Roesti Benedict: Place a potato pancake on each of 4 plates. Layer with a slice of Brie, a slice of prosciutto, and a few arugula leaves. Top each portion with a poached egg. Pour a small ladle of hollandaise sauce over each so that the poached egg is covered. Serve immediately.

Banana Cafe

1215 Duval Street
Key West, FL 33040
(305) 294-7227
BANANACAFEKW.COM
Danny Dahon, Owner
Dominique Falkner, Executive Chef and Owner
Christopher Donnelly, Chef de Cuisine

In the shadow of a giant poster of the banana-clad, American-born, Folies Bergère dancer Josephine Baker, which hangs under the stairwell, Banana Cafe serves authentic French cuisine, prepared utilizing classic French techniques, with an American flair for using local ingredients. Both natives of France, owners Danny Dahon and Dominique Falkner, along with chef de cuisine Christopher Donnelly, have created a touch of Paris amid the sea of Duval Street shops and honky-tonks.

Falkner, a writer who has published six novels in France, described his culinary philosophy:

> You ask me how my cooking is different for the island. A friend once told me that I cook the way I write. Writing and cooking are my two greatest loves, and they are necessarily linked. I really believe that cooking, real cooking, is an extension of your personality. It is shaped by your personal history, by where you come from, what you've done, where you've been. This, to me, is primordial.

The cooking I am interested in today, others or mine, is one that reflects honesty towards who you are as a person and therefore as a chef. And even though my cooking has been shaped by the chefs who taught me techniques and methods at the numerous restaurants at which I have worked, abroad and in the States, what I like to cook today essentially comes from the spirit of my childhood and the village where I grew up outside of Lyon, considered the gastronomic capital of France.

Everything on my menu is there for a reason. I grew up with leek salad. I picked up goat cheese terrine from an incredible restaurant in central France. I ate *pommes a l'huile* every day on my lunch break in Paris. Salmon is a wink at my days in Norway. Smoked corn dressing comes from the years I lived in Wisconsin. Chicken basquaise is rustic French soul food at its best.

When I look back at my years at the stove, I realize that maturing as a chef has meant striving further and further towards simplicity of form and honesty of taste.

Judging from the packed tables from breakfast all the way through the dinner hour, every day of the week, Falkner's culinary philosophy is a winner.

Yellowtail Snapper in Citrus Sauce

(SERVES 4)

For the Parisian gnocchi:

6 tablespoons unsalted butter
¾ cup water
Salt
1 cup all-purpose flour
3 eggs
½ tablespoon minced fresh chives
½ tablespoon chopped fresh parsley
½ tablespoon chopped fresh tarragon
1 tablespoon Dijon mustard
½ cup shredded Parmesan cheese
Freshly ground black pepper
32 ounces chicken stock

For the citrus sauce, snapper, and accompaniments:

1 lemon
1 orange
1 grapefruit
3 tablespoons olive oil, divided
8 cherry tomatoes
½ pound (about 15) haricots verts
Salt and freshly ground black pepper
4 tablespoons butter, divided
4 cups Parisian gnocchi
¼ cup flour
4 (6-ounce) yellowtail snapper fillets, deboned
   and washed
2 tablespoons olive oil
½ cup pineapple juice
¼ cup capers

To make the gnocchi: Place the butter, water, and 1½ teaspoons salt in a large saucepan over medium heat. When butter has melted, remove saucepan from the heat and stir in flour with a wooden spoon until dough pulls away from the sides of the saucepan. Place dough in the bowl of an electric mixer. Using the paddle attachment, add the eggs one at a time. Fold in the chives, parsley, tarragon, mustard, and Parmesan cheese. Season with salt and pepper to taste and mix well.

Place chicken stock in a large saucepan and bring to a simmer over medium heat. Transfer dough to a piping bag. Working slowly in small batches, cut small segments of the dough directly into the simmering chicken stock. When the gnocchi floats, it is done. Remove gnocchi from stock with a slotted spoon and allow it to cool on a parchment-paper-lined baking sheet. (Makes about 100 pieces. Gnocchi can be made up to 24 hours ahead and stored in the refrigerator under a clean, dry towel or wrapped carefully and frozen. Defrost gnocchi before cooking.)

To prepare the citrus sauce, snapper, and accompaniments: Peel the lemon, orange, and grapefruit and carefully cut them into segments using a small, sharp paring knife. Work over a bowl so that you collect any escaping juices. Set fruit segments aside and reserve juices.

Place 1 tablespoon olive oil in a medium skillet over high heat. When oil is very hot, add cherry tomatoes and sauté just until they burst. Remove skillet from heat and set aside.

Bring a medium saucepan of heavily salted water to a boil over high heat. Add haricots verts and blanch for 2 minutes. Drain haricots verts, rinse with cold water, and drain again. Cut each haricot vert into 5 pieces. Season with salt and pepper to taste. Set aside.

Melt 2 tablespoons butter in a large skillet over medium heat. Add gnocchi and haricots verts and sauté until lightly browned, about 5 minutes. (Do not overcook or the gnocchi will get hard.) Remove from heat and set aside.

Mix flour and desired amount of salt and pepper on a dinner plate. Dredge both sides of snapper fillets in flour. Shake fillets to remove excess flour. Place 2 tablespoons olive oil in a large nonstick skillet over high heat. When oil is hot, add the fish fillets and cook on each side for 3 minutes. Remove fillets from the skillet and place on a baking sheet. Cover with aluminum foil and set aside.

Add the pineapple juice to the skillet and place over high heat for 3 minutes. Add the citrus segments, reserved juices, and capers and cook for another 3 minutes. Add 2 tablespoons butter and reduce heat to low. Return fillets to the skillet and cook for 1 minute per side.

To assemble: Heap one-quarter of the gnocchi/haricots verts mixture in the center of each of 4 dinner plates. Top each with a snapper fillet and 2 cherry tomatoes. Ladle the citrus sauce and fruit segments around fillets on each plate.

Tuna Tartare

(SERVES 4)

For the key lime dressing:

1 tablespoon honey
½ cup key lime juice
1½ cups extra-virgin olive oil
Salt and freshly ground black pepper

For the soy-lime dressing:

½ teaspoon fresh minced ginger
½ cup soy sauce
1 clove garlic
Zest of 1 lime
Juice of 2 limes
3 jalapeños, seeded
½ tablespoon miso
2 tablespoons honey
1 cup canola oil
½ cup toasted sesame oil
Sea salt and freshly ground black pepper

For the sweet peppers in escabeche:

1½ cups champagne vinegar
½ yellow bell pepper, thinly sliced
½ red bell pepper, thinly sliced
½ green bell pepper, thinly sliced
1 shallot, sliced
1 clove garlic, sliced
½ bouquet garni
½ cup olive oil
Salt and freshly ground black pepper to taste

For the balsamic reduction:

2 cups balsamic vinegar

For the wasabi cream:

1 tablespoon wasabi powder
1 cup sour cream
½ cup heavy cream

For the tuna:

2 radishes, sliced very thin
¼ cup key lime dressing
1 pound fresh sushi-grade yellowfin or bluefin tuna,
    cut into ¼-inch cubes
½ cup sweet peppers, removed from escabeche
    and cut into ¼-inch cubes
1 shallot, finely diced
2 tablespoons chopped chives
½ cup soy-lime dressing
Salt and freshly ground black pepper to taste

½ cup seaweed salad
4 teaspoons domestic caviar

To make the key lime dressing: Whisk honey and lime juice together in a medium bowl, then slowly whisk in the olive oil. Season with salt and pepper to taste. Transfer to a covered container and refrigerate until needed.

To make the soy-lime dressing: Place all the ingredients except the oils and salt and pepper in a blender and pulse to mix well. With the blender on slow speed, slowly add canola oil to emulsify ingredients, then slowly add sesame oil until smooth. Season with sea salt and pepper to taste. Transfer to a covered container and refrigerate until needed.

To prepare the sweet peppers in escabeche: Bring vinegar to a boil in a large skillet over medium heat. Add peppers, shallots, garlic, and bouquet garni. Cook, stirring frequently, until peppers are soft. Remove from heat and stir in olive oil. Season with salt and pepper to taste. Transfer to a covered container and refrigerate until needed. Bring to room temperature before using.

To make the balsamic reduction: Place vinegar in a small saucepan over medium heat and simmer until it is a syrupy consistency. Place in a covered container and store for up to 3 months at room temperature.

To make the wasabi cream: Whisk wasabi powder, sour cream, and heavy cream together in a medium bowl until smooth. Transfer to a plastic squirt bottle and refrigerate until needed.

To prepare the tuna: Place radishes in a medium bowl with ¼ cup key lime dressing. Mix well and allow radishes to marinate for ½ hour. Place tuna, sweet peppers, shallots, chives, and ½ cup soy-lime dressing in a salad bowl and toss to combine. Season with salt and pepper to taste.

To assemble: Drizzle balsamic reduction and wasabi cream on each of 4 plates in a crisscross pattern. For each plate, arrange a tuna "tower" using a 2-inch-wide ring mold. Center ring mold on plate, and place one-quarter of the tuna mixture in the mold. Ease the mold off the tower, taking care not to press down on the tartare so that the tartare retains its juices. (Towers will be about 2 inches tall.)

Drain radishes. Top each tartare tower with one-quarter of the seaweed salad, one-quarter of the radishes, and 1 teaspoon caviar.

Better Than Sex,
A Dessert Restaurant

926 Simonton Street
Key West, FL 33040
(305) 296-8102
BETTERTHANSEXKEYWEST.COM
Len and Dani Johnson, Owners
Dani Johnson, Baker

"Dessert was what my mother and I bonded over the most when I was a kid," recalls diminutive Dani Johnson of her self-professed idyllic childhood. "I have very fond memories based on family togetherness and food." But, majoring in advertising and public relations in college, Dani never planned on being a baker.

One night in 2002, shortly after Dani and Len married and moved to Key West from Orlando, recalls Dani, "Len said, 'I want something sweet to eat.' Being the new wife, I was excited to blow him away and impress him, so I made him a fully decorated, two-layer Oreo cream cake. His words were, 'Wow, if you can do this, what else can you do?' That was all I needed to hear."

With day jobs as a bartender and a concierge, the couple secretly planned a dessert restaurant for five years. Dani devised binders full of new dessert recipes; Len worked on the business plan. They stumbled upon the restaurant's name in a magazine. "Better Than Sex just made sense," says Dani. "Dessert has no nutritional value. You don't need it; you only want it. So there's nothing to it but a good time!" She adds, "We said, 'Let's roll with this and all the innuendoes that go with it.'"

They first opened Better Than Sex on a shoestring budget in a small restaurant on Petronia Street in 2008. "I call it 'design on a dime,'" says Dani. "Chairs and tables were from Goodwill or the side of the road." She found four chandeliers at a thrift store for $41. Fabric came from Ross or Walmart. But with imagination, elbow grease, feng shui, and Dani's incredible desserts, it all came together and became an instant success. By 2012 they outgrew funky Petronia Street and moved "uptown."

With a sexy decor of red, gold, and black, and walls punctuated with provocative yet tasteful art, the dining room of Better Than Sex is so dimly lit, patrons are provided with little flashlights to read the menus. "It's mysterious and romantic," says Dani. "It makes people relax and feel like they are the only ones in the restaurant."

"Everything about our concept is a risk and is different," states Dani. Signature drinks are paired with caramel or chocolate. For Choco-Cab, the rim of the glass is dipped in warm chocolate (it drips down the side), then filled with red wine. The idea is lick (chocolate), sip (wine), lick, sip, lick, sip. And the desserts . . . oh, the desserts! Picture Missionary Crisp, Tongue Bath Truffle, Peanut Butter Perversion, or Between My Velvet Sheets. The only things better than the dessert names and their decadent flavor combos are the written descriptions. Sex Addict anyone?

SEX ADDICT

(SERVES 16 FULL-SIZE DESSERTS OR 32 TEASERS)

For the bread layer:

Baker's Joy

1-pound loaf sourdough bread, rough-cut into
    1-inch cubes

10 ounces frozen strawberries (no added juices
    or sugar)

10 ounces white chocolate bar, chopped

¼ teaspoon ground nutmeg, optional

For the custard filling:

6 eggs

3¼ cups heavy whipping cream, divided

⅓ cup butter, melted

¼ teaspoon salt

12 ounces white chocolate chips

¾ cup sugar

1 teaspoon pure vanilla extract

For plating:

Ice cream, sorbet, or frozen yogurt

16 chocolate-dipped strawberries

To prepare the bread layer: Spray a 9 x 13-inch baking pan generously with Baker's Joy. Place bread cubes in greased pan and sprinkle strawberries on top. Sprinkle white chocolate chunks evenly atop bread and strawberries. Sprinkle with nutmeg, if desired.

To prepare the custard filling: In the large bowl of an electric mixer, beat eggs until fluffy. Place 1¼ cups heavy cream, butter, and salt in a medium saucepan over medium heat. Bring to a rolling boil, then remove pan from heat. Add white chocolate chips and sugar. Stir with a whisk until chocolate chips melt and sugar dissolves. Gradually whisk in remaining 2 cups heavy cream. Slowly stir chocolate/cream mixture into the whipped eggs. Stir in vanilla extract.

To assemble the bread pudding: Slowly pour custard mixture over bread mixture in baking pan, working from the outside in. Then, using a fork, press down on the bread pudding, making sure to cover all the bread cubes with the custard mixture. Cover and chill at least 2 hours or overnight.

To bake the bread pudding: Preheat oven to 325°F. Place uncovered bread pudding on an aluminum foil–lined baking sheet. Bake 70–80 minutes or until an instant-read thermometer reads 180°F when inserted in the center. (If you want to prevent browning, cover the pan very loosely with foil before putting it in the oven, being careful not to let the foil touch the top of the bread pudding. Leave foil on for the first 50 minutes, then remove foil and continue baking for the remaining 20–30 minutes.) Cool bread pudding on a wire rack for at least 45 minutes.

To serve: When bread pudding is firm, cut into 8 squares. Remove each square from pan to a cutting board. Cut each square into 2 triangles to equal 16 triangles. If you desire smaller pieces, cut each triangle in half again. (You'll have 32 smaller servings.) Serve with your favorite ice cream, sorbet, or frozen yogurt and top with a chocolate-dipped strawberry.

CONCH REPUBLIC SEAFOOD COMPANY

631 GREENE STREET
KEY WEST, FL 33040
(305) 294-4403
CONCHREPUBLICSEAFOOD.COM
ERIC WHITTEN, EXECUTIVE CHEF

"I think our atmosphere is unmatched anywhere on the island," says executive chef Eric Whitten about Conch Republic Seafood Company, which sits aside the docks at Key West Historic Seaport. "Our eighty-foot bar is the largest in Key West, and the view is awesome. It's hard to beat dining or having a cocktail only a few feet from the water and watching the sunset."

Conch Republic Seafood Company (CRSC) stands on property that was once the Singleton Fish House and Ice Plant, where each day shrimp boats unloaded their catch. In the warehouse— now the main dining room of the restaurant— hundreds of workers toiled at long tables, beheading the shrimp before packing them for shipment.

Far from Key West Bight, Whitten grew up in a small South Texas town and was addicted to watching *Great Chefs* on television. "I was impressed by what you are able to do with food and how you can manipulate it into something so much more," he says. "I started cooking as a fry cook at sixteen and progressed. A lot just came naturally to me."

After attending culinary school in Corpus Christi and cooking in a fine-dining establishment in his hometown for six years, at age twenty-two "I bought a ticket, packed two bags, and here I am, eight years later!" Whitten exclaims. "It's an easy place to like, very laid-back and easygoing, and the water is amazing."

Staying true to its history, CRSC specializes in fresh seafood. Whitten keeps his cuisine traditional as far as technique, but adds Caribbean influences "to give it an island twist." "I like to start with ingredient flavor profiles and see which ones complement each other," he says, "then start building a dish from there." "I like clean, tight dishes," he continues. "I'm a believer in sticking to fundamentals. But that doesn't mean you can't think outside of the box."

Whitten advises the home cook to keep experimenting and not get intimidated by anything. "If it turns out wrong, at the end of the day it's food, not the end of the world!"

BLACKENED SCALLOPS WITH RISOTTO-STYLE ISRAELI COUSCOUS

(SERVES 2)

For the couscous:

1¼ cups water
1 cup Israeli couscous
1 cup heavy cream
½ cup shredded Parmesan cheese
Salt and freshly ground black pepper

For the saffron-leek cream sauce:

1 tablespoon butter
½ cup chopped leeks
1 tablespoon chopped garlic
½ cup white wine
¼ tablespoon saffron threads
2 cups heavy cream
Salt and freshly ground black pepper to taste

For the bok choy:

4 baby bok choy
¼ cup vegetable oil
Salt to taste

For the scallops:

8 (U-10) diver scallops
¼ cup blackening seasoning (Paul Prudhomme
    Blackened Redfish Seasoning recommended)
¼ cup vegetable oil

To prepare the couscous: Bring water to a boil in a medium saucepan over medium-high heat. Add couscous and boil for 8–10 minutes, or until couscous is tender. Remove from heat. Place cream in a medium saucepan over medium heat and bring to a simmer. Add couscous and Parmesan cheese. Stir continuously until cheese is completely melted. Add salt and pepper to taste. Set aside.

To make the saffron-leek cream sauce: Melt butter in a sauté pan over medium heat. Add leeks and garlic and sauté until leeks are tender. Stir in wine and saffron and cook, stirring occasionally, until reduced by half. Add cream and cook, stirring often, until reduced by half. Add salt and pepper to taste. Reduce heat to low, cover, and keep sauce warm until serving.

To prepare the bok choy: Cut bok choy in half lengthwise and wash thoroughly. Place a sauté pan over medium-heat heat. Add vegetable oil and bok choy and stir-fry until boy choy is crisp-tender. Add salt to taste. Set aside.

To prepare the scallops: Coat scallops with blackening seasoning. Place sauté pan over high heat. When pan is hot, add oil. Place scallops in pan and cook for 1–2 minutes per side, or until medium.

To assemble: Place a scoop of risotto couscous in the middle of each plate. Arrange bok choy so that it leans over the couscous. Place 4 scallops around bok choy on each plate. Drizzle saffron-leek cream sauce atop scallops.

Key West Pink Shrimp with Vera Cruz Sauce

(SERVES 6)

½ cup butter

1 jalapeño, seeded and chopped

1 green bell pepper, chopped

1 sweet onion, like Vidalia, chopped

½ tablespoon chopped garlic

2¼ pounds shrimp (any size), peeled and deveined

2 (8-ounce) cans tomato sauce

¼ cup capers, rinsed and drained

3 tablespoons chopped fresh cilantro

1 tablespoon cumin

1 teaspoon paprika

1 teaspoon salt

1 teaspoon black pepper

½ teaspoon white pepper

½ teaspoon dried thyme

¼ teaspoon dried oregano

1 (6-ounce) package instant yellow rice

Melt butter in a large skillet over medium-high heat. Add jalapeños, bell peppers, onions, and garlic and sauté until tender. Reduce heat to medium. Add shrimp and cook for 5 minutes or until shrimp turn pink.

Stir in tomato sauce, capers, cilantro, cumin, paprika, salt, black and white peppers, thyme, and oregano. Bring to a boil. Reduce heat to low and simmer, uncovered, for 20 minutes or until slightly thickened.

Meanwhile, cook rice following package instructions. Cover saucepan and keep rice warm on low heat until ready to serve.

Place a scoop of rice on each of 6 dinner plates. Top rice with shrimp and Vera Cruz sauce.

Stormy Waters

(SERVES 1)

1½ ounces Bacardi Orange (or other orange-flavored rum)

½ ounce Sailor Jerry (or other spiced rum)

3 ounces ginger beer

2 drops bitters

3 ounces club soda

½ slice orange

½ slice lemon

Fill a 14-ounce tall glass with ice. Pour rums, ginger beer, bitters, and club soda into a cocktail shaker and shake vigorously. Pour over ice and garnish rim of glass with lemon and orange slices. (These can be squeezed into the drink for added flavor.)

Oft a rowdy little city with more bars than churches, Key West has hosted its fair share of characters over the centuries, from booze smugglers to drug runners to hard-drinking literaries like Ernest Hemingway. Bellying up to the bar before noon or partying until dawn is de rigueur in this, the southernmost watering hole in the continental United States. Four of Key West's most iconic drinking establishments—Sloppy Joe's Bar, Schooner Wharf Bar, the Green Parrot, and Hog's Breath Saloon—have been enduring favorites for decades.

Sloppy Joe's Bar

201 DUVAL STREET
KEY WEST, FL 33040
(305) 294-5717
SLOPPYJOES.COM

Joe Russell shut down his illegal Front Street speakeasy the day Prohibition was repealed, December 5, 1933, and opened up the Blind Pig, a come-as-you-are gambling hall with fifteen-cent whiskey and ten-cent gin. His good friend and frequent patron, Ernest Hemingway, talked Russell into renaming his saloon Sloppy Joe's, after Hemingway's favorite Havana haunt.

In 1937, when Russell's landlord raised the bar's rent from three dollars to four, Russell picked up and moved the saloon—literally—to its present Duval Street location. Legend has it that customers picked up their drinks and as much furniture as they could carry and set up service at the new place without missing a sip. Its jalousie doors wide open by 9:00 a.m., Sloppy fans still drink it all in.

SLOPPY JOE'S MOJITO

(SERVES 1)

¼ ounce simple syrup
2 lime wedges
3 mint leaves
1½ ounces Bacardi Silver (light) rum
Club soda

Pour simple syrup into a cocktail shaker. Squeeze lime juice into shaker and add mint leaves. Muddle* contents of the shaker with a muddler or the handle of a wooden spoon. Add rum. Fill shaker with ice and shake the ingredients. Pour into a tall glass. Top off the drink with club soda. Serve immediately.

*To muddle means to simply bruise or gently pound the lime and mint leaves to release their juices and essence.

Schooner Wharf Bar

202 WILLIAM STREET
KEY WEST, FL 33040
(305) 292-3302
SCHOONERWHARF.COM

Owned by Paul and Evalena Worthington, who sailed into Key West Bight in 1984 aboard a 1926 classic schooner, the Schooner Wharf Bar is the centerpiece of Key West Historic Seaport. Originally serving spirits aboard the schooner *Diamante*, the bar eventually moved ashore, where it now enjoys a panoramic view of the yacht-and-schooner-filled harbor.

The bar is home to the 130-foot *Western Union*, one of last working schooners built in the United States, as well as a replica of the 139-foot schooner *America*, which won the first America's Cup in England in 1851. The schooners share center stage with musical storytellers, magicians, and live music bands. The late broadcaster Charles Kuralt once said, "This must be the center of the universe!"

FROZEN MANGO MINT MARGARITA

(SERVES 1)

¾ ounce Sauza tequila
½ ounce triple sec
Splash of mango puree
Splash of sour mix or lemonade
Small splash of lime juice
¼ ounce Crème de Menthe
Sprig of fresh mint
Thin half-slice of lime

Place a glassful of ice in a blender. Add tequila, triple sec, mango puree, sour mix, and lime juice. Pulse until well blended. (Add more ice if necessary.) Pour into a margarita glass. Drizzle Crème de Menthe over top of drink. Garnish with a sprig of mint on top and a slice of lime on the rim of the glass.

Green Parrot Bar

601 WHITEHEAD STREET
KEY WEST, FL 33040
(305) 294-6133
GREENPARROT.COM

Said to be equal parts honky-tonk, dive bar, and locals joint, the Green Parrot bills itself as "a sunny place for shady people!" Started as a grocery store in 1890, where locals enjoyed rum, cigars, and jamming Latin music in the back room, the place evolved into the Brown Derby Bar after World War II, for decades attracting sailors stationed in Key West.

By the 1970s, hippies, bikers, and nomads frequented the saloon, whose name had by then been changed to the Green Parrot. Shrimpers and drug smugglers came next, turning the bar into a "shit-kickin' honky-tonk." Music, real and raw, still reverberates from the Parrot, and the bar self-professes to be "a place of hijinks and misadventures, a jury of non-judging peers, and a ragged council of friends."

GREEN PARROT
ROOT BEER BARREL

(SIGNATURE DRINK, SERVES 1)

Place a shot glass inside a rocks glass.

Fill the shot glass with chilled Root Beer Schnapps.

Fill the surrounding rocks glass with beer, preferably lager, to the rim of the shot glass. Drink all at once!

Hog's Breath Saloon

400 FRONT STREET
KEY WEST, FL 33040
(305) 296-4222
HOGSBREATHKEYWEST.COM

Jerry Dorminy's grandmother used to say, "Bad breath is better than no breath at all!" The owner of Hog's Breath Saloon morphed her words into the bar's motto, "Hog's breath is better than no breath at all," which emblazons T-shirts acquired by nearly every drinker who has passed through the Key West watering hole since it opened in 1976.

Known for its laid-back atmosphere and fantastic live music, such as Kenny Chesney's acoustical jam in May of 2013, Hog's Breath hosts epic events like the annual Homemade Bikini Contest and Hair of the Hog Leather and Lace Bloody Mary Party. Mostly, the Hog Heads just like to kick back, drink and nosh a little, buy a T-shirt, and listen to the music.

WORLD FAMOUS HOG'S BREATH SALOON KEY LIME SHOOTER

(SERVES 2)

2 ounces silver rum
2 ounces Liquor 43*
1 ounce sour mix
1 ounce orange juice
½ ounce Rose's lime juice
½ ounce half-and-half

Fill a cocktail shaker with ice. Add all the ingredients and shake well. Strain into two shot glasses or martini glasses or serve over ice as cocktails.

*Liquor 43 is a Spanish liqueur made from citrus and fruit juices, flavored with vanilla and other herbs and spices, a total of 43 different flavors blended in all.

Cuban Coffee Queen

284 Margaret Street
Key West, FL 33040
(305) 294-7787
cubancoffeequeen.com
Marius Venter, Owner
Michelle Ellis, Manager

The unassuming, 200-square-foot shanty building emblazoned with a colorful Cuban mural might be easy to overlook, if not for the dozens of people lined up in front of its walk-up order window. Cuban Coffee Queen, sitting in a small corner of Key West Historic Seaport, attracts a loyal following of locals and tourists alike. "We open at 6:30 a.m.," says Michelle Ellis, the eatery's manager. "And since we serve breakfast and lunch all day until 8 p.m., it's not unusual for, say, boat captains to order both." She goes on, "We have people who come here every single day."

Owned by South African–born Marius Venter since 2011, Cuban Coffee Queen was

the brainchild of Key West chef Paul Menta, who traveled to Havana to explore how to make authentic Cuban food. As the story goes, Menta met an old Cuban woman who taught him the secrets of preparing authentic café con leche, bucci, and the country's signature sandwiches. He called her "the coffee queen."

"Cuban Coffee Queen is the only Cuban restaurant in Key West that does slow-roasted pork, which is cooked overnight," says Venter. Adds Ellis, "If you come by here in the middle of the night, you can smell it." Although Venter and Ellis—themselves both chefs—have tweaked the original recipes to keep them vibrant, the cuisine is still authentically Cuban.

"We sold 10,577 Cuban Mix sandwiches in 2013," says Ellis, "and 76,000 café con leches. Mind-blowing numbers when you get right down to it." Queen's Cuban coffee recipes remain closely guarded secrets, but Venter credits the superior quality of their beans, which are from Nicaragua, for setting them apart from the competition. "I am fascinated with the coffee industry," he says. "I go to coffee expos and we do blind tastings here all the time, in search of the very best coffee that is out there."

Nothing on Coffee Queen's menu is more than seven dollars. Says Venter, "We don't charge much money, but we keep the quality really high." Adds Ellis, "And we taste-test the Cuban Mix sandwiches elsewhere, so we know ours is the best!"

Cuban Mix Sandwich

(ROASTED PORK MAKES ABOUT 40 [4-OUNCE] PORTIONS)

For the roasted pork:

1 (6–9 pound) boneless pork shoulder butt
⅓ cup cumin
⅓ cup Badia Complete Seasoning
¼ cup adobo dry seasoning
2 cups peeled, whole garlic cloves
2 cups Badia Mojo Marinade
4 bay leaves
1 small onion, sliced

For 4 sandwiches:

4 (8-inch) pieces of Cuban bread
Mayonnaise
Yellow mustard
Sliced Swiss cheese
Thinly sliced deli ham

Sliced onions
Shredded lettuce
Sliced tomatoes
Sliced dill pickles

To prepare the pork: Preheat oven to 300°F. Place pork in a large roaster. Mix cumin, Badia seasoning, and adobo seasoning in a small bowl. Rub mixture atop pork. Place garlic and mojo marinade in a blender and pulse until smooth. Pour marinade over pork. Add water to 1 inch in the bottom of the pan. Add bay leaves and sliced onions atop pork. Cover pan and roast pork for at least 12 hours, or until it is soft and falling apart.

Discard fatty pieces and the majority of the liquid. Shred the pork using 2 forks. (Pork is so soft at

this point that it basically shreds itself.) Transfer about 1 pound shredded pork to a slow cooker with a little bit of the juice. Hold on warm until serving. (Refrigerate or freeze remaining pork for later use. Reheat in a slow cooker on low setting before serving.)

To assemble 4 sandwiches: Slice Cuban bread loaf, crosswise, into 8-inch pieces. Cut each piece in half, lengthwise. Lay bread open. Spread both cut sides with mayonnaise and mustard. On the top half of the bread, place a layer of cheese. On the bottom half, place a layer of ham, then a layer of onions. Place about 4 ounces roasted pork atop the onions. (Squeeze out some of the juice so the sandwich does not get soggy.) Finally add a layer each of lettuce, tomatoes, and pickles. Place top half of bread on sandwich and place it in a sandwich press (450°F) for 1–2 minutes, until the bread is slightly toasted. (If you don't have a Cuban sandwich press, you can use a George Forman electric grill or a panini press.)

Garbo's Grill

603 Greene Street
Key West, FL 33040
(305) 304-3004
GARBOSGRILLKW.COM
Kenna and Eli Pancamo, Chefs and Owners

Eli and Kenna Pancamo finish each other's sentences. Maybe because they have been a couple for thirteen years. Or maybe because they work together every day, side by side, in a five-by-eight-foot food cart, their wildly popular eatery, Garbo's Grill.

Although they loved to cook, Eli and Kenna never did so professionally before buying the Greene Street food cart in 2011. "We both worked front-of-the-house in restaurants," says Kenna, "but we'd do dinner parties for friends." "And try out new ideas on them," finishes Eli.

Eli dreamed of having a little burrito shop, and they explored the possibilities. When a brick-and-mortar establishment proved too costly and scary for the novice entrepreneurs, they jumped at the opportunity to buy Garbo's, which already had a following. "The original owner had just three things on the menu," says Eli. "We expanded it to ten."

They prep in a commercial kitchen commissary. "A cubbyhole, really," explains Eli. Everything is made fresh daily, and when they run out, they run out. Knowing Garbo's is open from 11:30 a.m. to 3:00 p.m., repeat customers come early to make sure they can get their favorites. Cooking in a shoebox is a finely choreographed culinary dance.

Three people, seven cold bins, coolers, garbage pails, sink, grill, assembly counter, cash register . . . all in that tiny space. But at Garbo's Grill, magic happens.

The Pancamos have pared down the menu so that they can offer creative specials. The Korean Bulgogi Tacos, Cayo Fish Sandwich, and Umami Burger are perennial favorites. "When we started out," says Eli, "I told customers, 'If you don't think that is the best burger you've ever had, I'll pay for it.' I've never paid for a burger!"

Each sandwich concoction utilizes an unusual combination of ingredients, infusing the palate with sweet, savory, and heat essences in each bite. The grilled ten-ounce burger, for instance, is topped with applewood-smoked bacon, steamed heirloom tomato, and melted smoked chipotle Gouda cheese and is served on a brioche bun. The grilled mahi in the Cayo sandwich is dressed with fresh mango, red cabbage, sliced jalapeños, cilantro, and onions and topped with Garbo's special, secret Caribbean sauce.

"We have one character who eats here every single day," says Kenna. Eli adds, "It is just so awesome that this worked!"

Korean Bulgogi Tacos

(MAKES 10–15 TACOS)

For the short ribs:

3 pounds beef short ribs, off the bone
1 cup soy sauce
½ cup dark brown sugar
⅓ cup mirin
¼ cup sesame oil
6 cloves garlic, peeled
6 scallions, cut into 1-inch pieces
2 teaspoons peeled, chopped fresh gingerroot

For the soy-lime dressing:

Juice of 2 limes
¼ cup soy sauce
2 tablespoons mirin
2 tablespoons Sriracha
2 tablespoons extra-virgin olive oil

For the Korean-style slaw:

3 cups coarsely chopped napa cabbage
1 cup matchstick-cut daikon
6 scallions, diced
3 tablespoons chopped cilantro

For the taco assembly:

10–15 yellow corn tortillas
Sriracha

To prepare the short ribs: Cut off any excess fat from the short ribs, then thinly slice the beef. Cut the beef slices into 1½-inch pieces. Place in a ziplock bag.

Place soy sauce, dark brown sugar, mirin, sesame oil, garlic, scallions, and gingerroot in a blender. Process until smooth. Pour half the marinade over the short ribs in the ziplock bag. Close bag and refrigerate short ribs for 3 hours or up to 24 hours. Place remaining marinade in a small saucepan over medium heat and cook it, stirring occasionally, until mixture has reduced and is thick. Place in a covered container and refrigerate until needed.

To make the soy-lime dressing: In a small bowl, whisk together lime juice, soy sauce, mirin, and Sriracha. Slowly whisk in olive oil. Cover and refrigerate until needed.

To make the slaw: Toss cabbage, daikon, scallions, and cilantro together in a medium bowl. Cover and refrigerate until needed.

To cook: Remove short ribs from marinade. Heat a griddle or large sauté pan on high heat. Place short ribs on griddle and cook for 2–3 minutes. Flip meat and cook an additional 3 minutes. Wrap meat in foil and set aside.

Place tortillas on griddle for 45 seconds. Flip tortillas and cook for another 45 seconds, then remove tortillas to a plate.

To assemble tacos: Place a spoonful of slaw in the middle of each tortilla. Drizzle it with soy-lime dressing. Place a spoonful of short rib meat atop slaw. Drizzle with thickened marinade sauce and, for additional kick, extra Sriracha. Fold taco in half and serve immediately.

Glazed Donuts

420 Eaton Street
Key West, FL 33040
(305) 294-9142
glazeddonutskw.com
Jonathan and Megan Pidgeon, Bakers and Owners

Perhaps the youngest owners of a food establishment in Key West, Jonathan and Megan Pidgeon, both in their late twenties, take the art of making donuts to the next stratosphere. Why donuts? "Because Megan has the most insane sweet tooth you have ever seen," quips Jonathan. "Seriously," says Megan, "growing up in Texas we had a donut shop every mile. I love donuts, and Key West did not have a donut shop."

Jonathan and Megan met and dated at the Culinary Institute of America in New York. Call them savory and sweet—he trained in culinary, she in baking and pastry. After graduating in 2007, the couple embarked on separate career paths for a while. Jonathan ran a barbecue company in his native Virginia, but, not partial to cold winters, in 2009 he headed to the Keys—no job, no place to live, all his "crap" in his truck. He landed at the BlackFin Bistro and worked his way up to executive chef.

Meanwhile, Megan headed to California, working as a pastry chef at Charlie Palmer's Dry Creek Kitchen and also with the acclaimed Nicole Plue in Napa Valley. A 2010

encounter with cheesemaking convinced her to briefly move to Vermont to try her hand at it, but disillusionment, the approaching cold winter, and Jonathan convinced her that moving to the Keys was a better option.

The couple married in 2011, and after intense collaboration, on April 8, 2012, their first baby, Glazed Donuts, was born. "It's the only child we are interested in having for the next few years," Jonathan jokes. Megan is the chief donut maker. Jonathan does the first morning batch of frying, then runs the front of the house and handles the coffee and smoothie orders, as she creates batch after batch of fresh, hot donuts.

"Baking and pastry are more science," says Jonathan. "Savory is more theory."

"I can look at a batch of dough and know by looking at it exactly what was mis-scaled, based on how it behaves," says Megan. The Pidgeons make everything from scratch, including all their donut fillings, glazes, and frostings, even the sprinkles, as well as their smoothie syrups. They try to source all their tropical fruits from South Florida.

Each donut (a whopping four inches in diameter) is a gustatory work of art, a blank canvas for the Pidgeons' creativity. They designed the Roasted Pineapple Brûlée donut as a takeoff on pineapple upside-down cake. "It was the first donut that really blew us away," states Jonathan. But as the Orchid Brûlée, St. Patrick's Day Black and Tan, Coconut Easter Egg, and Fantasy Fest Strawbooby prove, it was not the last.

Roasted Pineapple Brûlée Donuts

(MAKES 12 DONUTS)

For the glaze and garnish:

1 fresh pineapple
1 cup granulated sugar, divided
½ vanilla bean pod
1 cup simple syrup*
2 pounds confectioners' sugar

For the donuts:

1 tablespoon plus ¾ teaspoon yeast
1¼ cups plus ⅓ teaspoon warm tap water
6 tablespoons butter, softened
4 cups all-purpose flour, divided
½ teaspoon nutmeg
2 tablespoons sugar
3 tablespoons nonfat dry milk powder
1¾ teaspoons plus ⅛ teaspoon baking powder
1⅓ teaspoons salt
Canola oil for frying

To prepare the pineapple and make the glaze:
Preheat oven to 325°F. Carefully remove the entire rind of the pineapple with a serrated knife and slice the pineapple into even ¼-inch slices. (One pineapple should yield 19–22 slices.) Using the donut cutter, cut the core and edges off the pineapple slices. Discard the cores and reserve the cut-off edge scraps.

Place the pineapple rounds on a parchment-paper-lined baking sheet and sprinkle them with ¼ cup granulated sugar. Place the cut-off pineapple scraps and the vanilla bean onto another parchment-paper-lined baking sheet. Sprinkle with ¼ cup granulated sugar. Place both trays in the oven and roast for 1 hour. Remove trays from oven and allow to cool.

Fry pineapple rounds in a deep-fat fryer at 375°F until they are golden brown. Remove slices and place on a cooling rack until needed.

Scrape vanilla beans out of pod. Place vanilla beans, 1 cup roasted pineapple scraps, and simple syrup in a blender and puree. Transfer puree to the large bowl of an electric mixer. Slowly mix confectioners' sugar until smooth and well blended. Set aside until needed.

To make the donuts: Place yeast and water in the large bowl of an electric mixer and mix for 30 seconds with the dough hook attachment. Add butter, 3⅔ cups flour, nutmeg, sugar, milk powder, baking powder, and salt. Mix on low speed for 5 minutes. Stop mixer and scrape edges of bowl. Continue mixing on medium speed for an additional 5 minutes.

Lightly flour a flat surface with some of the remaining ⅓ cup flour. Remove the dough from the mixer and form into a ball on the floured surface. Cover dough lightly with plastic wrap and allow it to proof at room temperature for 20–30 minutes. (The dough is ready to roll out when you start to see air bubbles and the dough has not quite doubled in size.)

Roll out the dough to ½ inch thick. Cut into donuts with a donut cutter (3-inch diameter). Lightly flour twelve 4-inch squares of parchment paper. Place donuts on parchment squares. (This way, when you are ready to fry the donuts, you can just slide them into the hot oil.)

Proof the donuts for a final time by placing them on a baking sheet in a cold oven with a large casserole dish of boiling water (about a gallon) placed on the rack below. (You can also proof the donuts at room temperature, lightly covering

them with plastic wrap, but it will take longer.) Shut the oven door and after 20 minutes of proofing, check donuts. They are ready to fry when they have doubled in size.

Meanwhile, heat canola oil to 375°F in a deep-fat fryer, following manufacturer's instructions. Once donuts have doubled in size, slide 2–3 donuts at a time into the fryer, removing the parchment squares. Using long wooden chopsticks, turn the donuts until they are golden brown, about 45 seconds per side. Remove donuts from oil using a spider utensil (a wide, shallow wire-mesh basket on a long handle). You can also remove the donuts using tongs, if you do it very, very gently.

To assemble the donuts: Cover hands with disposable gloves. Working one by one, quickly place the pineapple rounds atop the hot donuts and dip them into the pineapple glaze. (You may have to hold onto the pineapple round and re-center it after removing it from the glaze.) Place glazed donuts on a cooling rack atop a baking sheet. Using the remaining ½ cup granulated sugar, evenly coat the glazed donuts with sugar and brûlée them with a kitchen blowtorch. (You can repeat this process up to three times for more crunch.) Allow donuts to cool for 3–4 minutes and enjoy immediately.

Chef Megan's instructions for making simple syrup: Place ⅔ cup sugar and ⅓ cup water in a medium saucepan over medium-high heat. When sugar has dissolved, remove from heat and allow syrup to cool.

Half Shell Raw Bar

231 Margaret Street
Key West, FL 33040
(305) 294-7496
HALFSHELLRAWBAR.COM
Tommy Radziejewski, Executive Chef

Wallpapered with metal license plates donated by patrons from all over the nation, Half Shell Raw Bar exudes the casual, laid-back vibes of old Key West. Situated on the docks of Key West Bight, Half Shell offers perhaps the freshest seafood in Key West—the fishing fleet unloads its catch a few yards from the iconic establishment and adjacent Half Shell Fish Market.

While locals and tourists have long called Half Shell a favorite, the place hit superstar status in 2013 when country singer Kenny Chesney showcased its interior on the cover of his *Life on a Rock* album, illustrating the song "When I See This Bar." Visible are the license plates, extensive beer taps, its vintage sailfish sculpture, and a row of stools that now have become a tourist attraction in their own right.

Executive chef Tommy Radziejewski brings his own Conch pedigree to Half Shell Raw Bar. Born in Key West, he says he "shadowed my mother's every move in the kitchen." "That's what sparked my interest in food," he adds. What made him obsessed with food, however, was a trip to Las Vegas when he was twenty-one. "I got to meet some great chefs and eat at some awesome restaurants," he recalls.

While he has trained at some of the best restaurants in Key West, Radziejewski credits Michael Schultz (director of operations for owner Pat Croce's group of Key West restaurants) with being his mentor. "I have learned tons from Michael," he says, "and from my mother." His philosophy for the cuisine at Half Shell and for the home cook as well is to "use fresh ingredients and keep it simple, but don't be afraid to think outside the box."

And while Half Shell is a great place to kick back, swig a beer, eat freshly shucked oysters, play darts, and listen to live music, it also may just offer a Chesney sighting from time to time.

RED CONCH CHOWDER

(SERVES 8–10)

½ pound ground salt pork
1 yellow onion, diced
1 green bell pepper, diced
3 tablespoons minced garlic
¾ pound ground conch, drained
½ cup tomato paste
32 ounces water
16 ounces stewed tomatoes
1½ teaspoons crushed red pepper
1½ teaspoons poultry seasoning
1½ teaspoons dried oregano
1 teaspoon dried basil
1 teaspoon dried thyme
1 teaspoon white pepper
1 bay leaf
2 pounds peeled potatoes, cut into small dice
Cilantro leaves

Brown salt pork in a large saucepan over medium-high heat. Drain grease and discard. Add onions, peppers, and garlic to the pan and sauté with the salt pork, stirring frequently, until vegetables are transparent, about 15–20 minutes. Add conch, reduce heat to medium-low, and sauté for 30 minutes, stirring occasionally. Add tomato paste and water and stir to combine. Cook for 30 minutes more, stirring occasionally.

Place stewed tomatoes in a blender and pulse to break them down. Add tomatoes, crushed red pepper, poultry seasoning, oregano, basil, thyme, white pepper, and bay leaf to the pot and stir to combine. Cook for 30–45 minutes, stirring occasionally. Add potatoes and cook for an additional 20–25 minutes. Transfer chowder to a container and refrigerate uncovered until totally cooled, then cover container. (Chowder freezes well and can be stored this way for several months.)

To serve: Remove bay leaf from chowder. Reheat chowder in a large saucepan over low heat. Serve in shallow soup bowls and garnish with cilantro leaves.

Sunset takes center stage in the twilight hours in the Florida Keys. Almost like a pagan ritual, visitors and residents alike jockey for an unobstructed vantage point from which to watch the smoldering orange ball ooze into the sea like a sphere of molten lava.

Flotillas of small boats drift anchorless in the Gulf waters . . . waiting. Travelers pull their autos off the Overseas Highway and stand at water's edge, mouths agape as their eyes fixate on the horizon. But nowhere in the Keys is the Sun God more worshipped at day's end than at Mallory Square in Key West, where fire-eaters, aerial acrobats, sword swallowers, and musicians compete with Mother Nature.

Once the sun starts to sink into the sea, all eyes lock onto the fireball in search of the optical phenomena, the green flash. The rare sighting of the emerald-colored flash just as the sun melts into the water lasts only a second or less. What causes a green flash? Certain atmospheric conditions cause the light from the sun to separate into different color bands, just like in a prism. Blue and green wavelengths are refracted the most, so the setting sun may appear to have a blue-green fringe on its top edge. The glare of the sun hides the fringe until all but the upper rim is blocked by the horizon, and a brief spot of green flashes as the sun disappears into the sea.

At this point on land, however, the party usually has just started to heat up. One of the best spots to drink, nosh, listen to live music, and watch the sunset is Sunset Pier, at Zero Duval Street, adjacent to Ocean Key House and the Mallory Square sunset celebration. A string of umbrella-topped tables pepper the narrow pier, all facing directly out at the harbor with an unparalleled sunset vista.

Sunset Pier

While the buskers play to the crowds at Mallory Square, ceremonial Keys sunset watchers at Sunset Pier can sip a Pusser's Painkiller, nibble on Cuban Pork Empanadas, and use this ten-point secret rating scale to judge the show:

- Score five points if the sun sets at all, because that means you are alive.
- Add: One point for pre-glow (the reflection of the sun streaks across the water).
- Add: One point if you see the bottom of the sun touch the horizon.
- Add: One point if the top of the sun touches the horizon.
- Add: One point if you see an afterglow (the sky turns pastel colors).
- Add: One point if you enjoy the company you keep while watching the sunset.
- Score a bonus point if a sailboat, bird, or cloud moves in front of the sun as its sets.
- The sighting of the green flash is an automatic 10.

Cuban Pork Empanadas
with Guava Barbecue Sauce

(MAKES 30–40 EMPANADAS)

For the guava barbecue sauce:

2 quarts (64 ounces) bottled barbecue sauce
2 cups canned guava marmalade

For the roasted pork:

1 (4-pound) pork butt roast
Salt
3 cups bottled mojo marinade sauce, such as Badia

For the empanadas:

2 (10-count) packages empanada dough
Canola oil for frying

To make the guava barbecue sauce: Mix barbecue sauce and guava marmalade in a large bowl. Transfer to a covered container and refrigerate until needed. (Sauce can be refrigerated for 1 week or frozen for up to 1 month.)

To prepare the roasted pork: Salt pork butt and place it in a roasting pan or oven-safe casserole dish. Allow it to sit at room temperature for 1 hour.

Preheat oven to 425°F. Add mojo sauce to pan and cover pan tightly with foil. Place covered roast in oven and immediately reduce heat to 200°F. Roast pork for 4 hours. When pork is done, remove it from oven and allow it to cool for 1 hour at room temperature. Shred meat using a fork.

To prepare the empanadas: Place shredded pork in a large bowl and toss with 2 cups guava barbecue sauce. Cut each circle of empanada dough in half, creating 2 half-moon shapes. (You will have 40 half-moon pieces.) Place 1 tablespoon pork mixture into the center of each half-moon piece of empanada dough and fold dough in half. Using a fork, press down firmly on the edges to seal them tightly. Place assembled empanadas on a tray or baking sheet.

Place canola oil in a deep-fat fryer to manufacturer's instructions. Heat oil to 350°F. (If you don't have a deep-fat fryer, you will need to use a high-walled sauté pan. Fill with oil to about one-third from the top and heat to 350°F on the stove.) Place empanadas in the hot oil and fry until they are golden brown. (If using a sauté pan, you will need to flip the empanadas over to finish the other side.) Remove empanadas from oil with a slotted spoon and place on a paper-towel-lined plate.

To plate and serve: Reheat remaining guava barbecue sauce in a medium saucepan over low heat. Transfer to a serving bowl. Place bowl in the center of a large platter. Arrange empanadas on platter, around the bowl, and allow diners to dip empanadas in sauce to serve themselves. (Empanadas can be made ahead and refrigerated up to 4 days or frozen up to 1 month. Reheat room-temperature empanadas in a 350°F oven for 20 minutes before serving.)

SUNSET PIER'S PUSSER'S PAINKILLER

(SERVES 1)

1¼ ounces Pusser's rum
4 ounces pineapple juice
1 ounce orange juice
1 ounce coconut cream
Nutmeg

Fill a cocktail shaker with ice. Add rum, pineapple and orange juices, and coconut cream. Shake well and pour into a tall glass. Sprinkle with nutmeg. Serve at once.

Hot Tin Roof

OCEAN KEY RESORT & SPA
ZERO DUVAL STREET
KEY WEST, FL 33040
(305) 296-7701
OCEANKEY.COM
JASON WESTPHAL, EXECUTIVE CHEF

Jason Westphal credits his beautiful baby girl as the impetus to become a more inspired and in-tune chef. Once labeled "Key West's bad boy chef," Westphal says those days are gone. "No more of the wild chef nights out, filled with beer and cigs," he says. "I have

become more of listener and a helper to my employees," he continues. "Now I want to be labeled as just a good all-around chef."

The talented executive chef at Ocean Key Resort's prestigious Hot Tin Roof, Westphal grew up in a close-knit Ohio family. "I was a mischievous kid who didn't like to do a lot of things I was told to do," he confesses. "I really liked doing my own thing. But from a young age I was always intrigued with both preparing and eating food."

Westphal started his culinary journey on the pantry station at Moxie the Restaurant in Beachwood, Ohio, and worked his way up the line for about seven years before being promoted to sous chef at Moxie's sister restaurant, Red the Steakhouse in Cleveland. And like so many snowbirds before him, Westphal jumped at the chance to trade the cold and snow for the palm trees and beaches of Miami, becoming executive sous chef at Red the Steakhouse in Miami.

After a stint at Miami's primo seafood restaurant, Altamare, and a few visits to the Keys to unwind, fish, and relax, Westphal decided island life might be more his style. His restaurant, Hot Tin Roof, sits astride the Gulf of Mexico and enjoys one of the best sunset venues in Key West.

The kid who liked to do his own thing has evolved into the chef who dares to be different in his culinary creations. The fresh, local seafood of the Keys inspires Westphal. He considers it a blank canvas on which he can pair flavors that will complement each other. "If you follow your heart, you will always make good food," he advises. "I'm always looking for that something that will wow the guest."

Coconut Chorizo Stew Topped with Grilled Grouper

(SERVES 8)

For the stew:

1 pound unsalted butter

3 pieces dried chorizo, cut into ⅛-inch rounds

3 carrots, cut into medium dice

2 large yellow onions, cut into medium dice

5 stalks celery, cut into small dice

2 red bell peppers, cut into medium dice

2 green bell peppers, cut into medium dice

3 ears corn, kernels removed and reserved

4 cups (1 pound) flour

7 (13.5-ounce) cans unsweetened coconut milk

3 tablespoons Spanish paprika

Salt and freshly ground black pepper

For the grouper:

8 (8-ounce) black grouper fillets

Kosher salt

Olive oil

To make the coconut chorizo stew: Place butter in a large pot over high heat. When butter begins to melt, add chorizo. Cook chorizo for 5–10 minutes. (Butter will turn a dark red.) Add carrots, onions, celery, bell peppers, and corn kernels and cook until onions are translucent. Reduce heat to medium-low and stir in flour. Stir constantly until no clumps remain, with no flour burning to the bottom of the pot. Add half the coconut milk and stir until mixture is smooth. Add remainder of the coconut milk and paprika. Increase heat to medium-high and bring mixture to a simmer, stirring occasionally. Season with salt and pepper to taste.

To prepare the grouper: Preheat grill on high heat. Lightly season fillets with kosher salt and rub each with a little olive oil. Place fillets on grill and cook for 3–5 minutes. (Do not try to turn fillets during this time or they will stick to the grill.) Flip the fillets and cook for an additional 3–5 minutes, until just cooked through and flaky. (For thick fillets, after the first 3- to 5-minute sear, turn half the grill to off. Place a piece of aluminum foil on the cool side of the grill and transfer fillets to foil, close the lid, and finish cooking until just cooked through and flaky.)

To plate and serve: Place 8 ounces of coconut stew in each of 8 large-rimmed bowls. Top each with a grilled grouper fillet.

Hot Tin Huevos Rancheros

(SERVES 6)

3 tablespoons butter

6 (6-inch) flour tortillas

1 pound fresh chorizo sausage, cooked, drained, and crumbled

3 cups grated Manchego cheese

6 large eggs

1½ cups salsa

2 cups pico de gallo

6 tablespoons sour cream

1 tablespoon fresh cilantro leaves

Preheat oven to 375°F. Butter the 6 cups of a maxi-muffin pan (½ tablespoon for each cup). Place a tortilla neatly in each hole. Divide the chorizo evenly among the 6 tortilla-lined cups. Sprinkle cheese evenly among the cups. Break an egg into each cup. Add about ¼ cup salsa to each cup. Place in the oven for 20–25 minutes or until eggs are cooked to desired temperature (yolk sunny-side up or cooked all the way through).

Remove muffin pan from oven and allow huevos rancheros to cool slightly. Gently lift each ranchero from its cup and place it on an individual plate. Garnish each with pico de gallo and top each with 1 tablespoon sour cream and a sprinkling of cilantro leaves. Serve immediately.

LATITUDES RESTAURANT

245 FRONT STREET
SUNSET KEY
KEY WEST, FL 33040
(305) 292-5300
WESTINSUNSETKEYCOTTAGES.COM/LATITUDES-KEY-WEST
TODD HOLENDER, EXECUTIVE CHEF

Todd Holender always knew he would be a chef. It's in his DNA. "It feels like second nature," he says. "It was never a conscious decision." Holender grew up in Sunrise, Florida, around food service and restaurant kitchens. "My dad was a chef," he explains. "My first job was in the kitchen and I just kept progressing."

Holender, executive chef of the exquisite Latitudes restaurant on Sunset Key, lists four things of great importance to his culinary pursuits: travel, learning, change, and pushing the envelope. He attended two culinary schools in Orlando before honing his craft in the field in restaurants from North Carolina to Utah to Alaska to Maine. "Travel is learning," he states. "You get a little piece from every chef you work with, every state you are in, every experience you have. You never stop learning. I am still learning."

When Holender joined Ocean Properties, Ltd., which owns Key West's Westin and Sunset Key, he discovered a means to balance his four prerogatives. He traveled from state to state, opening or transitioning the corporation's varied hotel restaurants, and took a taste of every place he went, learned from every chef he met. "You always have to reinvent yourself, learn new techniques, keep pushing yourself," he says.

Down-to-earth and engaging, with striking blue eyes, Holender opened the new Latitudes in 2010. A sleek outside-inside plantation-style restaurant, set on the beach amid swaying palms and the lapping waters of the Gulf of Mexico, Latitudes, under Holender's vision and tutelage, pushes the culinary limits just a little bit, so that diners can try something new but not be out of their comfort zone.

"We are seafood-driven here in the Keys," he says. "I look for product availability. I ask myself, 'What can I do different with this?' and I try to get everyone in the kitchen involved in creating new dishes." The menu changes often. Holender credits this and other changes, "like new plates or new chairs" or doing big weddings and events, with keeping things fresh for him at Latitudes.

Asked what is the most special feature of his restaurant, Holender modestly mentions the ambience, the boat ride from Key West to Sunset Key, and the beautiful sunsets, not his award-winning, cutting-edge cuisine. "It's just cooking," he states. "I'm not Steve Jobs."

Sweet Potato Crusted Grouper with Truffle Cauliflower Puree and Roasted Garlic & Thyme Cream Sauce

(SERVES 4)

For the garlic puree:

2 large heads of garlic
¾ cup extra-virgin olive oil
Salt and freshly ground black pepper

For the thyme cream sauce:

4 tablespoons butter, divided
1 shallot, finely chopped
Salt
1 cup white wine
2 cups heavy cream
Freshly ground black pepper
Juice of 1 lemon
1 tablespoon roasted garlic puree
1 sprig thyme, chopped

For the vegetables:

1 head white cauliflower, rinsed and cut
    into large chunks
2 cups whole milk
Salt and freshly ground black pepper
1 tablespoon white truffle oil, optional
8 spears asparagus
1 head Romanesco or purple cauliflower,
    rinsed and cut into florets
1 tablespoon butter

For the grouper fillets:

1 sweet potato
1 russet potato
½ cup canola oil
1 egg, beaten

1 cup flour, seasoned with salt and freshly
    ground black pepper
4 (6–8 ounce) black grouper fillets

To make the garlic puree: Preheat oven to 350°F. Cut top ¼ inch off the heads of garlic to expose cloves. Place garlic in a small baking dish. Add oil, sprinkle with salt and pepper to taste, and toss to coat. Turn garlic cut-side up and cover tightly with aluminum foil. Bake until garlic skins are golden brown and cloves are tender, about 55 minutes.

Remove from oven, remove foil, and allow garlic to cool. Squeeze garlic cloves from skins. Mash garlic with a fork and transfer puree to a covered container. Refrigerate until needed.

To make the thyme cream sauce: Melt 2 tablespoons butter in a medium saucepan over medium heat. Add shallots and a sprinkling of salt and cook until shallots are soft and tender. Add wine and cook until reduced by three-quarters, stirring occasionally. Add cream and cook until reduced by half, stirring occasionally. Season with salt and pepper to taste. Stir in lemon juice and roasted garlic puree.

Turn off heat and add remaining 2 tablespoons butter, a little at a time, stirring until butter is incorporated. Stir in thyme, cover, and set aside on a warming burner or a warm spot on the stove.

To prepare the vegetables: Place white cauliflower in a pot of boiling water and cook over medium-high heat until fork tender. Drain cauliflower and place in a blender. Add milk, salt

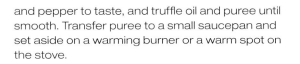

and pepper to taste, and truffle oil and puree until smooth. Transfer puree to a small saucepan and set aside on a warming burner or a warm spot on the stove.

Bring another large pot of water to a boil over medium-high heat. Fill a large bowl half full with ice, half with water. Place asparagus in boiling water for 45 seconds. Remove asparagus with tongs and place in a strainer. Submerge asparagus-filled strainer in ice water. Remove strainer from ice water and drain asparagus on paper towels.

Add purple cauliflower to boiling water for about 90 seconds. Remove cauliflower to a strainer and submerge cauliflower-filled strainer in ice water. Remove from ice water and drain cauliflower on paper towels. Reserve vegetables.

Before serving: Melt 1 tablespoon butter in a medium sauté pan over medium heat. Add reserved purple cauliflower and asparagus and cook just until heated through. Season with salt and pepper to taste.

To prepare the grouper fillets: Place a box grater in a large bowl. Shred sweet and white potatoes on grater. Rinse and drain potatoes until water runs clear. Drain potatoes in a colander, then squeeze water out of them using a clean dish towel. Place potatoes on paper towels to dry. Once dry, transfer to a shallow bowl.

Place oil in a large sauté pan over medium heat. Place beaten egg and seasoned flour in separate shallow bowls. Working one fillet at a time, flour one side of each fillet and brush a generous

amount of the egg wash over flour. Press fillet, egg-washed side down, into the potato mix.

Carefully place fish, potato side down, into the pan. Repeat with remaining fillets. When potatoes are cooked and become crispy, turn fish and continue to cook until fillets are cooked through. Season potato side of fillets with salt and pepper to taste. Remove fillets from oil and drain on paper towels, potato side up.

To assemble: Place a spoonful of thyme cream sauce (about 2 ounces) in the center of each of 4 dinner plates. Place a grouper fillet atop sauce, potato side up. Place a spoonful of cauliflower puree on each plate next to the grouper and run a spoon through it to form a teardrop. Place equal portions of purple cauliflower and asparagus on the opposite side of the grouper. Serve immediately.

Butter Poached Florida Lobster Tail with Creamy Herb Polenta, Champagne Beurre Blanc, Caviar & Asparagus

(SERVES 4)

For the beurre blanc sauce:

¼ cup champagne vinegar
2 cups champagne
1 shallot, chopped
1 bay leaf
½ cup heavy cream
2 sticks butter
Juice of 1 lemon
1 sprig thyme, chopped
Salt and freshly ground black pepper

For the polenta:

2 cups chicken or vegetable stock
1 cup whole milk
1 cup polenta cornmeal
4 tablespoons butter
Salt and freshly ground black pepper

For the lobster tails:

4 (6–8 ounce) Florida lobster tails, removed
    from shells whole

1 tablespoon sea salt
2 sticks (8 ounces) butter

For the asparagus:

16 spears asparagus, trimmed and peeled (half green
    and half white, if available)
1 tablespoon butter or olive oil
Salt and freshly ground black pepper

Caviar (whatever your budget allows)
1 bunch chives, cut fine

To make the beurre blanc sauce: Place vinegar, champagne, shallots, and bay leaf in a medium saucepan over medium to medium-high heat and reduce, stirring occasionally, until almost dry. Stir in cream and reduce by three-quarters. Remove saucepan from heat and add butter, 1 tablespoon at a time, stirring constantly, until all the butter is incorporated. Add lemon juice and thyme and season with salt and pepper to taste. Cover saucepan and reserve sauce on a warming burner or a warm spot on the stove.

To prepare the polenta: Place stock and milk in a large saucepan over medium-high heat and bring to a boil. Reduce heat to low and slowly add the polenta, stirring constantly until thickened. Stir in butter and season with salt and pepper to taste. Set aside on a warming burner or a warm place on the stove.

To cook the lobsters: On the counter, lay out four 12 x 12-inch pieces of plastic wrap. Place a lobster tail in the center of each square. Season both sides of tails with sea salt. For each portion, tuck tail following its natural curve until rounded. Cut each stick of butter in half and flatten like a patty. Place 1 butter patty atop each rounded lobster tail. Wrap each lobster tail tightly in plastic wrap.

Fill a medium pot halfway with water and bring to a simmer (180°F). Add wrapped lobster tails to the pot and place a heavy plate atop them so that tails are submerged. Cook lobster tails for 10–15 minutes. Stir lobster packets gently with a wooden spoon every few minutes. When lobsters are cooked through (instant-read thermometer inserted in the center should read 145°F), remove them from the water and allow them to rest for a couple of minutes before removing the plastic wrap.

To prepare the asparagus: Bring a large pot of water to a boil over high heat. Fill a large bowl half with ice, half with water. Place asparagus in boiling water for 45 seconds. Drain in a strainer, then immediately submerge asparagus-filled strainer in ice water. Remove strainer and allow asparagus to rest.

Before serving, heat 1 tablespoon butter or olive oil in a medium sauté pan. Add asparagus and heat it through, tossing asparagus constantly. Season with salt and pepper to taste.

To assemble: Spoon ¼ cup polenta in a corner of each dinner plate. Put the tip of a spoon in the center of the polenta so that it touches the plate. Pull spoon through polenta to create a teardrop shape. Place 2 spears of white asparagus and 2 spears of green asparagus in the center of each plate. Unwrap lobster tails and place a tail atop asparagus on each plate. Top lobster with a spoonful of beurre blanc sauce and spoon some sauce around the plate. Top each lobster tail with 1 teaspoon caviar and sprinkle with chives.

LOUIE'S BACKYARD

700 WADDELL AVENUE
KEY WEST FL 33040
(305) 294-1061
LOUIESBACKYARD.COM
DOUG SHOOK, EXECUTIVE CHEF

"It never occurred to me to cook as a career," says Doug Shook. "I went to acting school in college." But life paved a different path for Shook, who has been executive chef at the acclaimed Louie's Backyard for twenty-nine years.

Shook left school at nineteen and headed to San Francisco, where he waited tables for years. "My experiences with people in the kitchens were not good," he remembers. But the Belgian lunch cook at a French bistro where he worked "was a sweetheart of a guy, the first person I'd encountered in the kitchen who wasn't just a total jerk! " says

Shook. When the salad girl quit, the chef pressed Shook into service. Then both the lunch cook and the dinner chef left, and the bistro's owners put Shook totally in charge. "I had only been in the kitchen for six months," he remarks.

Shook juggled the kitchen alone for two weeks, until a new chef was hired. "He was a mean Frenchman who wanted me gone immediately, but the owners said no," Shook remembered. "Because he was really lazy, he taught me everything he knew so that he wouldn't have to do it himself." A year later, at age twenty-three, Shook found himself executive chef of the bistro and on his way to a career in the kitchen.

Several years later Shook moved to Washington, DC, where he worked for a gifted caterer who was really adventurous with flavors and taught him global cuisines. But Shook hated DC, so in 1985 he headed to Key West, where he was introduced to the famed Norman Van Aken, then chef at Louie's Backyard. Shook was hired as lunch chef, and within two years he took over as executive chef when Van Aken moved on.

In the 1970s Louie Signorelli ran a little twelve-seat restaurant in the oceanfront backyard of his Victorian home on Waddell Street—the original Louie's Backyard. Phil and Pat Tenney bought the restaurant in 1983, expanding and renovating it into the jewel it is today. "This is only the third restaurant I've worked at in my life," Shook says with a laugh.

The genius behind Louie's award-winning cuisine modestly states, "This is not a solo act by any means. I have a great staff. We have developed a common sense of taste." Shook maintains relationships with several local fishermen, who supply Louie's needs directly. "Fish is the biggest percentage of food cost at the restaurant," says Shook, "so I fillet all the fish myself."

When creating new dishes, Shook puts tastes together in his head. "My style is to leave the pretension out of it and go for something that is good. I ask myself, 'Would my wife want to eat this?' If I can please her, I can please the world."

GRILLED LAMB RIB CHOPS WITH CAULIFLOWER-CHÈVRE PUREE & SUN-DRIED TOMATO RELISH

(SERVES 8)

For the sun-dried tomato relish:

½ cup sun-dried tomatoes, finely diced
1 large shallot, finely diced
2 cloves garlic, minced
½ cup snipped flat-leaf parsley
½ cup extra-virgin olive oil
½ teaspoon cracked black pepper
Zest of 1 lemon

For the cauliflower-chèvre puree:

1 head cauliflower
½ cup heavy cream
4 tablespoons butter
4 ounces chèvre cheese
Salt and freshly ground black pepper

For the chops:

16 (2-rib) lamb chops, cut from the rack
    (about 6 pounds)
Salt and freshly ground black pepper
2 tablespoons olive oil

To make the relish: Combine all the ingredients in a small bowl and stir until well blended. Transfer to a covered container and refrigerate until needed.

To make the cauliflower-chèvre puree: Place a large saucepan of salted water over medium-high heat and bring it to a simmer. Trim cauliflower and cut it into florets. Add cauliflower to water and simmer until tender. Drain thoroughly in a colander.

Place cooked cauliflower, cream, butter, and chèvre in a food processor and puree until smooth. Season with salt and pepper to taste. Transfer to a heatproof bowl and place on a warming burner or a warm place on the stove until needed.

To prepare the chops: Preheat a gas grill or prepare a charcoal grill fire to medium-hot. Season chops with salt and pepper to taste and brush them with olive oil. Grill chops for 5–7 minutes per side, until medium-rare. Remove chops from grill and set aside to rest for 5 minutes.

To plate and serve: Make a pool of cauliflower puree in the center of each of 8 dinner plates. Place 2 chops atop each pool of puree. Top each with an equal portion of sun-dried tomato relish and serve immediately.

CHOCOLATE BROWNIE CRÈME BRÛLÉE

(SERVES 8)

For the brownies:

6 tablespoons plus 1 teaspoon unsalted butter

9 ounces semisweet chocolate, chopped

1¼ cups sugar

½ teaspoon salt

1 teaspoon vanilla extract

3 extra-large eggs

6 tablespoons flour

For the custard:

4 cups heavy cream

1 vanilla bean

10 extra-large egg yolks

1 cup sugar, divided

To make the brownies: Preheat oven to 325°F. Grease a 9 x 13-inch baking dish with 1 teaspoon butter. Place chopped chocolate and 6 tablespoons butter into the top of a double boiler over simmering water. Stir until butter and chocolate are melted and smoothly combined. Stir in sugar, salt, and vanilla. Add the eggs one at a time, stirring between additions until smooth. Slowly stir in the flour until mixture is smooth and shiny.

Spread the batter in the prepared baking pan and bake for 35–40 minutes, until the edges of the brownies begin to pull away from the sides of the pan and the center is just firm. Do not overbake. Allow brownies to cool before cutting them into 2-inch squares.

To prepare the custard: Place cream in a 2-quart saucepan over medium heat. Split vanilla bean and scrape out seeds. Add the bean and seeds to the cream. Bring cream and vanilla to a simmer.

Whisk egg yolks and ½ cup sugar together in a large mixing bowl. Slowly pour simmering cream into the bowl, whisking constantly. Pour this custard back into the saucepan and place over medium heat. Cook custard, stirring constantly, until it thickens enough to coat a wooden spoon. (Don't allow the custard to boil.) Strain custard through a sieve into a clean bowl and refrigerate until it is thoroughly chilled.

To prepare the crème brûlée: Preheat oven to 325°F. Place a brownie in the bottom of each of eight 6-ounce custard cups, pressing down to make it stick to the bottom of the cup. Divide the custard equally among the cups, filling each to within ½ inch of the rim. Place the custard cups in a roasting pan and add hot water to the pan to reach halfway up the sides of the cups. Cover the pan with aluminum foil and cut several vents in the foil. Place the pan in the oven and bake for 35–45 minutes, until the custard is just set. Remove the custard cups from the water bath and refrigerate until completely cold.

To serve: Sprinkle 1 tablespoon sugar evenly over the top of each custard. Aim the flame of a kitchen blowtorch directly at the sugar until it melts, bubbles, and caramelizes. Serve immediately.

Martin's Restaurant

917 Duval Street
Key West, FL 33040
(305) 295-0111
MARTINSKEYWEST.COM
Martin Busam, Chef and Owner

Growing up in the Black Forest area of Germany, Martin Busam found himself in a restaurant kitchen at an early age. "My family operated a guesthouse and restaurant called Gasthaus zum Kreuz. My father and mother were both chefs, and my three brothers and I all had to help them in the kitchen."

Busam went on to do a three-year term of study to become a pastry chef. "I always say a pastry chef can cook, but a cook cannot make pastries," he says with his characteristic hearty laugh. Busam worked at several patisseries and owned his own small restaurant before leaving Germany to follow a friend to Key West.

"I opened Martin's Cafe in the guesthouse of Eden House on Fleming Street in 1990," Busam says. He moved the restaurant two times over the next eighteen years, ever expanding, to Grinnell Street and then Appelrouth Lane, before making the final hop to his present Duval Street location.

Along with his twin brother, Fritz, who came over from Germany to help with the front of the house, Busam completely transformed the existing building into a sleek

European bistro . . . linen-topped tables with crystal and fresh flowers, handmade wallpaper imprinted with real gold, goose-feather chandeliers made by a German artist, and Fritz's signature photographic artwork adorning the walls. The courtyard garden dining, also crystal and linen, sits among palms and tropical foliage.

"Up until now, I've always done all the cooking myself," says Busam. "Now I have another chef to help me," he says with a laugh, "but I still make all the pastries myself." At Christmas, Busam makes little marzipan cakes with a penny inside each for good luck, a German tradition he brought with him to Key West. While much of his German heritage is still evident, Busam describes his cuisine as more European with an island flair. His native Black Forest is influenced by neighboring France and Switzerland, he says. "I pull those influences into my cuisine."

GROUPER DIJON OVER CHAMPAGNE SAUERKRAUT

(SERVES 4)

For the sauerkraut:

4 tablespoons butter
¾ cup sliced shallots
3 tablespoons flour
4 cups canned sauerkraut, rinsed
    and drained
1 cup champagne

For the Dijon hollandaise sauce:

3 tablespoons dry Riesling wine
3 egg yolks
2 sticks butter
Splash of lemon juice
½ tablespoon fresh bread crumbs
¼ cup Dijon mustard
Salt and freshly ground black
    pepper

For the grouper:

¼ cup flour
Salt and freshly ground black
    pepper
4 (6-ounce) black grouper fillets
2 tablespoons butter

Melt butter in a large sauté pan over medium-high heat. Add shallots and sauté for 1–2 minutes. Stir in flour until well blended. Stir in sauerkraut and cook until it is warmed through, about 4–5 minutes. Add champagne and mix to bind the ingredients. Remove from heat, cover, and set aside on a warming tray or on a warm spot on the stove.

Place the bottom of a double boiler, half-filled with water, over medium-high heat. Place wine and egg yolks in the top of the double boiler. When water is hot, place top of double boiler over the water-filled bottom pan. Whisk wine and yolks until mixture begins to thicken. (If the sauce begins to break down or curdle, add 1 or 2 tablespoons boiling water to stabilize it.)

Add butter, a couple of tablespoons at a time, whisking constantly. When all the butter has been incorporated, add a splash of lemon juice. Stir in the bread crumbs and mustard and mix well. Season with salt and pepper to taste. Remove from heat, cover, and keep sauce warm on a warming tray or a warm spot on the stove.

Preheat broiler. Place flour on a large plate and add salt and pepper to taste. Dredge both sides of fish fillets in flour. Melt butter in a large ovenproof sauté pan over medium heat. (Use a pan large enough to hold the fillets in one layer.) Add fish fillets and sauté for 5 minutes. Gently turn fillets and sauté for an additional 4–5 minutes. Spoon Dijon hollandaise sauce over grouper fillets. Place sauté pan under the broiler for 1 minute or until the crust begins to brown.

Place equal portions of champagne sauerkraut in the center of each of 4 dinner plates. Top each with a Dijon-hollandaise-crusted grouper fillet and serve immediately.

Michaels Restaurant

532 Margaret Street
Key West, FL 33040
(305) 295-1300
MICHAELSKEYWEST.COM
Michael and Melanie Wilson, Owners
Michael Wilson, Executive Chef

Michael Wilson's appreciation of a medium-rare steak began in boyhood at a backyard barbecue with his father. "My dad said, 'When the juices stop coming out of the steak, you know it is ready,'" says Wilson with a laugh. "Dad cooked everything well done!" Spurning family advice, Wilson, a graduate of Illinois's Washburn Culinary School, instead learned about beef from the best.

Wilson joined Morton's Steakhouse in Chicago in 1984 as a line cook. At the end of his shift, he liked to hang around and watch the butcher, who taught Wilson how to break down a side of beef. Armed with his culinary talents and a solid knowledge of all cuts of beef, Wilson was promoted to chef, first at Morton's in Westchester, Illinois, then in Boston, Massachusetts, and finally was named the company's corporate chef, where, still in his early twenties, he opened nineteen new Morton's restaurants.

Wilson stayed with Morton's, based in Chicago, until 1995, at one point overseeing thirty-three restaurants in the burgeoning chain. But he was sick of the cold and the snow, so leaving his corporate job behind, he became chef at Morton's in West Palm Beach. There he met wife Melanie and together they transitioned to Key West, she as a waitress, Wilson as a chef.

In 1997, on a shoestring budget, the couple opened Michaels Restaurant. "Mel worked at Sloppy Joe's during the day and I worked at a breakfast spot," recalls Wilson. "We'd literally run home, shower, and work at Michaels at night. We couldn't afford to pay ourselves. We did the 'day job, dream job' juggling act for nine months to pay the bills until things took off."

And take off they did. Michaels' steaks are flown in from Allen Brothers in Chicago, the same company Wilson used to supply Morton's. "People told me I'd never make it opening a steak house in a town like Key West," says Wilson. "But I had to stay true to what I believed. Consistency and quality are the make-or-break factors in the restaurant business." His mentor, George Gangas, in whose Greek coffee shop Wilson worked as a teenager, gave him some sage advice that he has never forgotten: "If you're going to serve lumpy gravy, make sure you serve it every day." "And I serve lumpy gravy every day," Wilson jokes.

Small and intimate, Michaels Restaurant is an oasis of greenery, set in tropical gardens, inside and out. A nod to his roots, Wilson describes his cuisine as Midwestern comfort food with a flair. He likes to keep ingredients and flavors at three or four, max, on a plate. "Too many flavors overwhelms the palate," he advises.

SCALLOPS & BRIE WITH RUBY PORT REDUCTION

(SERVES 2)

6 ounces ruby port wine

1 tablespoon butter

1 small round Brie cheese (about 9 ounces)

⅛ cup all-purpose flour

Salt and freshly ground black pepper

6 (1½-ounce) dry-pack diver scallops

1 tablespoon olive oil

Place port in a sauté pan over high heat and cook until reduced by half. Add butter and stir until it melts. Set pan aside on a warming burner or a warm place on the stove.

Using a 1½-inch round cutter, cut Brie into 2 disks. Set aside.

Place flour on a plate and season with salt and pepper to taste. Lightly dust top and bottom of the scallops with seasoned flour. Place oil in a large sauté pan over medium-high heat. When oil is hot, add scallops and sear to a golden brown, about 1½ minutes per side.

To plate and serve: Place a disk of Brie in the center of each of 2 small plates. Place 3 scallops around each round of Brie. Pour half the ruby port reduction atop each portion of scallops and Brie. Serve immediately.

Key Lime Martini

(SERVES 1)

1½ ounces Stolichnaya Vanilla Vodka
1½ ounces Ke Ke Beach Key Lime Cream Liqueur
Splash of heavy cream
½ ounce key lime juice
1 wedge key lime
Graham cracker crumbs

Place vodka, liqueur, cream, and key lime juice in a cocktail shaker. Fill shaker with ice. Shake vigorously. Press key lime wedge around the rim of a martini glass. Place graham cracker crumbs on a small plate. Press rim of glass into crumbs. Pour drink into graham-cracker-lined glass, straining out ice cubes. Serve and enjoy!

WHITE STREET STATION

In February 2014 Michael and Melanie Wilson and partner Dennis Kelly opened a curbside gourmet food truck, White Street Station, at the corner of Truman Avenue and White Street. Offerings from the eight-by-sixteen-foot truck range from the decadent braised short rib and macaroni and cheese sandwich, to the healthy chickpea "chick"en salad with vegan mayonnaise on whole-grain bread, to the ethnic Bánh Mì sandwich with Kurobuta pork belly, country pate, pickled daikon, cilantro, cucumber, and carrots on a French baguette. Stand-up tables made from old ironing boards under a colorful canopy welcome those on the go for a quick bite. For updates visit face book.com/white streetstation.

New York Pasta Garden

1075 Duval Street, #2
Key West, FL 33040
(305) 292-1991
NEWYORKPASTAGARDEN.COM
John Gaddoniex and William Jordan, Owners
Ray Williams, Executive Chef

Ray Williams had retired by the time he was eighteen. "I was a fighter," he says, "until my body couldn't do it anymore." Williams started full-body kickboxing—taekwondo—in a gym in Philadelphia at age nine. "I grew up in bad neighborhoods," he says of his upbringing. "Fighting was a natural."

Williams was passionate about the sport, going on to win national titles eight years in a row and to compete in the Junior Olympics at age fourteen and the US Olympics at seventeen. Having to quit the sport after a series of debilitating injuries was a crushing blow for him. But being the fighter that he is, Williams turned to something else he loved: food.

"All the women in my family were these cooks who would make special stuff from the old country," he says of his German relatives. "I was always interested and fascinated with what they were doing." But it was in a little Italian restaurant in North Philly, San Remo, where Williams got his first kitchen job, sweeping floors. He worked himself up through every station in that kitchen and others in Philadelphia and then New York City. "I fell in love with Italian food," he says.

Williams packed up his worldly possessions and headed for the Keys, having secured a dream job as executive chef aboard a ninety-foot live-aboard dive yacht. "I was only on land two or three days a month," he remembers. "It was awesome." When the dive yacht business was sold in 2003 and he found himself out of a job, Williams joined the New York Pasta Garden culinary team. "There were a few guys ahead of me," he says, "so I started out on the line." Four years later he became executive chef.

New York Pasta Garden features a small crystal-and-linen, NYC-style bistro dining room indoors, as well as expansive outdoor garden dining nestled under a giant royal poinciana tree. (In the summer months the tree is a canopy of flamboyant red-orange blossoms.) "When you have a setting and atmosphere like this along with really great food, it fuses into something you won't forget," says Williams.

"We try to make this like a friendly New York City neighborhood restaurant," says Williams of the eatery, which is tucked away in Duval Square, hidden from the bustle of Duval and Simonton Streets. The pasta is made fresh every day and specials abound. "I'm always looking for new concepts," says Williams of his approach to creating new Italian-themed dishes. "I am as passionate about cooking as I was about kickboxing."

Seafood Lasagna Trescaline

(SERVES 12)

For the warm seafood base:

¼ cup canola oil
1 teaspoon chicken base
1 teaspoon clam base
1 teaspoon seafood base
¼ cup chopped garlic
¼ cup chopped white onions
½ cup chopped roasted red peppers
½ cup chiffonade-cut fresh spinach leaves
¼ cup capers
¼ cup chopped clams
¼ cup chopped shrimp
2 (7-ounce) Florida lobster tails, chopped into dice
1 (4-ounce) can crab claw meat
1 pound dry diver scallops, chopped
½ cup Chablis white wine
1 stick salted butter

For the cold ricotta base:

4 ounces minced clams
4 ounces chopped cooked shrimp
2 (10-ounce) cans crab claw meat
2 teaspoons blackening seasoning
1 teaspoon salt
1 teaspoon black pepper
1 teaspoon garlic powder
2 tomatoes, diced
½ cup Chablis white wine
3 pounds ricotta cheese
2 cups shredded mozzarella cheese
½ cup grated Romano cheese

For the seafood sauce:

¼ cup olive oil
1 teaspoon clam base
1 teaspoon seafood base
½ cup diced onions
¼ cup diced red bell peppers
1 (10-ounce) can blue crab claw meat
1 teaspoon garlic powder
1 teaspoon black pepper
1 teaspoon red pepper flakes
¼ cup capers
4 pints plus 3 ounces (67 ounces) heavy cream
¼ cup marinara sauce
2 cups grated Romano cheese

For the lasagna:

Canola oil
20 cooked lasagna sheets
1 pound shredded mozzarella
1 cup panko crumbs
12 large shrimp, peeled and deveined, tails intact
Blackening seasoning

To make the warm seafood base: Place canola oil in a large sauté pan over medium-high heat. When oil is hot, stir in chicken, clam, and seafood bases. Add garlic, onions, roasted red peppers, spinach, capers, clams, shrimp, lobster, crabmeat, scallops, and wine. Sauté for 10 minutes, stirring occasionally. Stir in butter, a little at a time, until melted and well blended. Set aside until needed.

To make the cold ricotta base: Mix clams, shrimp, and crabmeat in a large bowl. Toss with blackening seasoning, salt, pepper, and garlic powder. Stir in tomatoes, wine, and cheeses. Set aside until needed.

To make the seafood sauce: Place olive oil in a large saucepan over medium-high heat. When oil is hot, stir in clam and seafood bases. Add onions, bell peppers, and crabmeat. Stir in garlic powder, black pepper, red pepper flakes, and capers. Add cream, marinara sauce, and Romano cheese. Bring to a boil and cook, stirring frequently, until reduced and creamy. Remove from heat and set aside on a warm place on stove.

To prepare the lasagna: Preheat oven to 375°F. Place canola oil in a 12¾ x 10⅜ x 2⁹⁄₁₆-inch lasagna pan, just so that it covers the bottom. Place a layer of lasagna sheets in the pan. Spread half the cold ricotta base over lasagna sheets. Pour the warm seafood base atop ricotta base. Add another layer of lasagna sheets. Spread remaining ricotta mixture atop sheets. Place a final layer of lasagna sheets atop ricotta mixture. Top with shredded mozzarella. Sprinkle panko crumbs atop lasagna. Bake for 25 minutes, until lasagna is heated throughout and panko crumbs form a crust, browned around the edges.

Meanwhile, butterfly-cut the shrimp. Toss shrimp with a small amount of canola oil and season with blackening seasoning to taste. Place butterflied shrimp on a hot grill and cook, turning once, until no longer translucent and just cooked through. Remove from grill and set aside.

To plate and serve: Cut lasagna into 12 portions and place each in the center of a dinner plate. Ladle about 4 ounces seafood sauce atop each portion. Top each portion with a grilled shrimp, tail up. Serve immediately.

Nine One Five

915 Duval Street
Key West, FL 33040
(305) 296-0669
915duval.com
Stuart Kemp, Owner
Darren Robey, Executive Chef

One lunch hour in 1988, fed up with London weather, British-born Stuart Kemp, on a whim, signed up to wait tables on a cruise ship and was on his way to the Caribbean the next day. Eight months later, after a brief stop in Key West, he abandoned ship in Miami and headed back to the Keys. Kemp started bartending in Key West to support himself, a fortuitous career move, as it turned out.

After years spent bartending at Mangoes, Kemp opened his own nightclub, called Wax, in 1998. By 2002, having had enough of the witching hours, he sold the club and opened Nine One Five. "I've always loved food," he says. "I've loved spending my money in other people's restaurants. Still do!" Admittedly naive about the restaurant business, Kemp says he was "knife-edge of going under for five or six years," until everything took off.

Kemp's cuisine concept has always been "simple food that you don't cut corners with," and his executive chef, fellow-Brit Darren Robey, concurs. "People want to know what they are eating and where it is coming from," says Robey. "I don't want Nine One Five to be just another Key West restaurant. I want it to be seasonal, fresh, and all house-made," he says.

Classically trained in culinary school in England, but cooking his way up the line in San Francisco and the California wine country for years, Robey creates "seasonal rustic cuisine" with the farm-to-table approach. Trying to do seasonal cuisine while living on a rock frustrates many a Key West chef, and Robey is no exception. The Keys may sport a plethora of wonderful seafood but no gardens, and Robey had a bit of ingredient withdrawal at first. But if you try, he says, "you can make it happen."

Making everything from scratch contributes to the success of Nine One Five's cuisine. They prepare their own beef stock, Thai curry paste, and duck confit, for example. For the bar, Kemp makes his own tonic from Peruvian quinine bark, brews his own ginger beer, and prepares sour mixes from fresh-squeezed citrus.

Upstairs in the Point Five Lounge, Kemp added a pizza bar, installing a brick pizza oven and constructing the Dade County pine bar himself. "At Nine One Five we serve incredible food in a casual environment," says Kemp. "It could be served in a double-linen restaurant anywhere. It is of that quality." Robey adds, "I always want to push to make it better. I want people to say, 'Wow, that is a great dish!'"

Moroccan Lamb Loin with Vegetable Tagine

(SERVES 4)

For the lamb:

6 tablespoons extra-virgin olive oil
2 cloves garlic, minced
1 tablespoon lemon zest
1 teaspoon Spanish paprika
1 teaspoon ground coriander
½ teaspoon ground cumin
½ teaspoon freshly ground black pepper
1 teaspoon cayenne pepper
Pinch of saffron threads, crumbled
1 (3-inch) cinnamon stick
1 tablespoon kosher salt
4 (8-ounce) lamb loins
2 tablespoons canola oil

For the Greek lemon yogurt:

1 cup Greek yogurt
Zest of 1 lemon
¼ teaspoon cayenne
¼ teaspoon ground cumin

For the vegetable tagine:

1 cup whole almonds
¼ cup extra-virgin olive oil
1 onion, cut into ¼-inch dice
2 cloves garlic, minced
1 carrot, cut into ¼-inch dice
Zest of 1 lemon
2 teaspoons Spanish paprika
2 teaspoons ground coriander
1 teaspoon ground cumin
1 teaspoon freshly ground black pepper
¼ teaspoon cayenne pepper
Pinch of saffron threads
1 tablespoon tomato paste
2 cups chicken stock

2 cups canned chickpeas, rinsed and drained
1 cup pitted green olives, rinsed and drained
1 cup chopped flat-leaf parsley

For the garnishes:

Greek lemon yogurt
4 sprigs fresh parsley

To prepare the lamb: Mix olive oil, garlic, lemon zest, paprika, coriander, cumin, black pepper, cayenne pepper, saffron, cinnamon stick, and salt in a large bowl. Add lamb loins and toss until well coated with mixture. Cover and refrigerate for 4 hours.

To prepare the Greek yogurt: Mix yogurt, lemon zest, cayenne, and cumin in a small bowl. Cover and refrigerate until needed.

To make the vegetable tagine: Preheat oven to 350°F. Place almonds on a baking sheet and roast until golden brown, about 10 minutes. Remove from oven and set aside.

Place olive oil in a large, heavy, ovenproof saucepan over medium heat. When oil is hot, add onions and garlic and sauté, stirring occasionally, until golden. Add carrots, lemon zest, paprika,

coriander, cumin, black and cayenne peppers, and saffron and cook for 1 minute. Add tomato paste and stir to combine. Add chicken stock, chickpeas, almonds, and olives. Cover saucepan and place in oven for 45 minutes. Remove from oven and sprinkle with chopped parsley.

To cook the lamb: Remove lamb from marinade, place on paper towels, and pat dry. Place canola oil in a 10-inch skillet over medium-high heat. When oil is hot, add lamb loins and sear for 3 minutes on each side. Remove loins from pan and place on a cutting board. Allow lamb to rest for 5 minutes.

To plate and serve: Divide vegetable tagine among 4 dinner plates. Slice each lamb loin and place slices atop the tagine. Finish each serving with a dollop of Greek yogurt and a sprig of fresh parsley.

CRAB CAKES WITH FINGERLING POTATOES, ANDOUILLE SAUSAGE, ARTICHOKES & LEMON AIOLI

(SERVES 4)

For the crab cakes:

1 large egg yolk
1 tablespoon cider vinegar
1 tablespoon finely chopped onion
¼ cup chopped fresh flat-leaf parsley (leaves only), divided
1 teaspoon Tabasco sauce
½ teaspoon paprika
½ teaspoon chopped fresh thyme
Pinch of kosher salt
Dash of fresh ground black pepper
¼ cup olive oil
¼ cup sour cream

1 pound fresh Dungeness crabmeat, picked clean of shell and lightly squeezed if wet
4 cups panko bread crumbs
2 tablespoons canola oil

For the lemon aioli:

3 cloves garlic, chopped
1 large egg
1 tablespoon freshly squeezed lemon juice
1 tablespoon chopped fresh flat-leaf parsley
½ teaspoon salt
2 turns freshly ground black pepper
½ cup olive oil

For the artichokes, fingerling potatoes & Andouille sausage

8 baby artichokes

2 lemons, cut in half

12 fingerling potatoes, cleaned but not peeled

¼ cup extra-virgin olive oil

Salt

Freshly cracked black pepper

2 tablespoons canola oil

1 Andouille sausage, sliced

¼ cup chopped fresh flat-leaf parsley (leaves only)

To make the crab cakes: Place egg yolk, vinegar, onions, 5 teaspoons chopped parsley, Tabasco, paprika, thyme, salt, and pepper in a small food processor. Pulse to mince the vegetables and combine the ingredients. With motor running, slowly add oil through the feed tube until the mixture emulsifies and forms a thin mayonnaise. Transfer mayonnaise mixture to a large bowl and stir in sour cream, then carefully fold in crabmeat.

Gently form the mixture into 4 crab cakes, about 3 inches in diameter and ¾ inch thick. Place panko crumbs in a shallow container and stir in the remaining chopped parsley. Lightly coat both sides of the crab cakes with the panko. Transfer crab cakes to a plate, cover with plastic wrap, and refrigerate for 2 hours.

Place a large nonstick skillet over medium heat and add canola oil. When oil is hot, add crab cakes to the pan. Fry cakes for 4 minutes, until golden brown. Turn crab cakes with a spatula and fry for about 4 minutes more, until golden brown and heated through. Set aside.

To make the aioli: Combine garlic, egg, lemon juice, parsley, salt, and pepper in a food processor or blender and puree. Add oil in a slow stream and continue to process until the mixture has formed a thick emulsion. Set aside until needed.

To prepare the vegetables: Preheat oven to 400°F. Remove the tough outer leaves of the artichokes and trim the stems. Use a vegetable peeler to remove the tough outer green layer from the stem. Cut off the top third of each head to remove the tough ends of the leaves, then split each down the middle. (Rub artichokes with lemon as you work so they don't turn brown.) Cut the fingerling potatoes in half lengthways.

Place artichokes and potatoes in a medium bowl. Toss with olive oil and season with salt and pepper to taste. Transfer vegetables to a roasting pan and place in oven. Roast artichokes about 20 minutes, potatoes about 30 minutes.

Place canola oil in a medium skillet over medium heat. When oil is hot, add Andouille sausage slices and cook, stirring occasionally, until golden brown. Gently stir in potatoes and artichokes. Remove from heat and stir in parsley.

To plate and serve: Divide vegetable mixture among 4 dinner plates. Top each portion with a crab cake and finish with a drizzle of lemon aioli.

From *Top Chef* to *Hell's Kitchen*, television's reality cooking competitions pale in comparison to the show put on in the southernmost city every January. The culmination of a weeklong Food and Wine Festival, the Master Chef's Classic pits dozens of Key West's top chefs against each other in the categories of appetizer, entree, and dessert.

This popular charity event, proceeds of which have benefited MARC (Monroe Association for ReMARCable Citizens; see box in this sidebar) since 2004, unfolds outdoors along the stunningly beautiful waterfront harbor at the Westin Resort. Each chef, set up under a large canopy with little more than two banquet tables, a couple of portable stovetop burners, and one or two helpers, must prepare 425 tapas-size servings of each of their competing dishes.

At 2:00 p.m. a panel of six judges begins the blind tastings. Each entry is judged on creativity, presentation, and

taste. At promptly 4:00 p.m., the gates open and hundreds of hungry foodies descend upon the festivity and begin a whirlwind taste-testing of their own. (A People's Choice award joins the judges' first-, second-, and third-place verdicts in each category at the end of the evening.)

"The Master Chef's Classic is a blast, man," states Brendan Orr, executive chef at Roof Top Café. Orr, a multi-year winner who competes every year, echoes the sentiments of his competitive peers, "My super-talented crew and I get to create special dishes representative of our restaurant. It's fun."

Monroe Association for ReMARCable Citizens, Inc.

Since 1966 Monroe Association for ReMARCable Citizens, Inc., has served Florida Keys residents with intellectual disabilities, such as mental retardation, cerebral palsy, spina bifida, Prader-Willi syndrome, and traumatic brain injury sustained prior to age eighteen. The organization maintains residential group homes as well as adult day training facilities and an annual summer camp. MARC provides safe, healthy living environments with a sense of family for their clients. Their retail plant store gives clients a chance to learn about horticulture and helps them acquire the skills needed to run a business.

In addition, MARC provides individuals employment training and support, inclusion in community activities, and transportation to and from MARC-supported services, and maintains an on-call medical professional for emergency situations, twenty-four hours a day. They also offer temporary housing for clients in one of their group homes in the event of a family emergency.

The Key West Master Chef's Classic is one of MARC's major fund-raising events, held every year at the end of January. State and federal funding has been cut significantly in recent years, just as the needs of the county's ReMARCable citizens has increased. Consult MARC's website for donation information: marchouse.org.

Old Town Bakery

930 Eaton Street
Key West, FL 33040
(305) 396-7450
OLDTOWNBAKERYKEYWEST.COM
Niall Bowen, Baker and Owner

As he was emerging from a rather rough adolescence, Niall Bowen recalls his father telling him: "If you just pick one thing and stick with it, you can probably end up ahead of the game." So at seventeen, Bowen answered a help-wanted ad at a French pastry shop and stuck.

Bowen credits his mentor, Kevin Jones, master baker at Maxim's Patisserie in Newton, Massachusetts, with teaching him old-world baking techniques and igniting a passion for his craft. He learned to make absolutely everything from scratch using very traditional French methods.

From there, Bowen attended Johnson & Wales in Providence, Rhode Island, earning an associate's degree in baking and pastry arts, and he began working as a pastry chef in Atlanta and then back in Massachusetts before following a friend to the Florida Keys to work for a season. He landed a job as pastry chef at the prestigious Louie's Backyard, where he met his Polish wife, Ella, who was waiting tables. "It was a restaurant romance," he says.

The dream, however, was to have his own bakery. That dream was relegated to the back burner for a while when Hurricane Wilma flooded out his house in 2005 and destroyed most of the equipment he had been amassing for the bakery. But as his father so long ago advised, he stuck with it.

In May 2010 Bowen's dream became a reality. Old Town Bakery opened, serving breads and pastries to an immediately enthusiastic and loyal Key West following. "It

was two and a half years of nonstop eighteen-hour days, seven days a week," he says. Bowen has stuck with the traditional techniques he learned back at Maxim's. He uses a forty-year-old, eighty-quart Hobart mixer and an old metal balance scale of weights and measures. He rolls his dough with a rolling pin, not the oft-used sheeter. "You can really feel it with a rolling pin," he says "It's hard on your back and shoulders, but you can feel the temperature, the thickness, the gluten strength."

Bowen grinds almonds and hazelnuts in-house instead of using a commercial product. And he still creates the scones, Linzer tortes, sticky buns, and croissants exactly as he did back at Maxim's. "I try to avoid trends as much as possible," Bowen says, preferring instead to make authentic French pastry. "It's easy to impress someone with something they've never had before," he says. "The challenge is giving them something familiar that makes them say it was the best they ever had!'"

Gorgonzola-Walnut Baguettes

(MAKE 2 BAGUETTES)

5 cups unbleached bread flour, divided

1½ cups cold water

2 teaspoons kosher salt

½ ounce fresh compressed yeast

12–14 ounces ripe Gorgonzola cheese

2 cups walnut halves

Vegetable cooking spray

Cornmeal, optional

Mix 4 cups flour and water in a large bowl with a spoon until well blended. (There should be no lumps of dry flour.) Cover the bowl with a damp cloth and allow mixture to rest for 20 minutes.

Sprinkle some of the remaining flour on a flat surface and turn the dough out onto it. Knead in the salt thoroughly, then knead in the yeast. (Yeast should not be directly combined with salt, so mixing process requires these two stages.)

Knead the dough by hand, flouring the surface lightly only when necessary to keep the dough from sticking to the table. (If lots of flour is kneaded into the dough at this stage, the bread will dry out, so use just what you need.) Knead the dough until, when a small piece is cut off with

a sharp knife, it can be carefully stretched thin enough to see light through it without breaking. (This test shows that the gluten in the dough is properly and completely developed, giving the dough the elasticity that it needs to rise.)

Put the dough back into the large bowl and cover it with a damp cloth. Allow dough to rise at room temperature for 1 hour. It should rise to about one and a half times its size in that amount of time.

Punch the dough down to knock out most of the gases. Divide the dough in half, to make 2 baguettes. Form the 2 pieces of dough into balls and place them on a lightly floured baking sheet or cutting board. Cover with a damp cloth and allow them to rise again for about 40 minutes. (The dough should just about double in that time. If it has not, you can wait longer. The amount of rise is more important than the amount of time.)

Once the dough has risen to about double, take the dough balls, one at a time, to the table. (If the dough is quite sticky, flour the table slightly. If is not very sticky, don't flour the table, as it will make the formation of the loaf more difficult.)

For each loaf, stretch and pull the dough, without ripping, to form a rough rectangle shape with the length running left to right in front of you. Crumble 6–7 ounces of the Gorgonzola into chunks about ½ to 1 inch in size. Place the chunks across the middle of the dough rectangle. (The top and bottom edges should not have the cheese, as they will have to stick together and become the "seam" of the baguette.)

Spread 1 cup walnuts evenly around with the cheese. Starting at the long edge farthest away from you, roll the dough's edge down toward you, rolling the cheese and nuts up into the loaf. When the loaf is rolled up, push the "seam" down with your thumbs to seal it. Then roll the loaf back and forth on the table to elongate it. Roll it to the length of your baking sheet (the longer the pan, the better). Taper the ends of the loaf to a point.

Line baking sheet with parchment paper or silicon baking paper. Coat paper lightly with vegetable cooking spray. (Dust the paper with cornmeal if you like the texture and flavor it imparts to the bread.) Place both loaves on the baking sheet, seam-side down. Lightly coat the top of the loaves with vegetable cooking spray. Cover the loaves loosely with plastic wrap. (This is to stop the dough from drying out while it rises, which happens rapidly when the dough is uncovered. You need to seal off the dough from the outside air without pinning down the dough with the plastic wrap by wrapping it too tightly. The pan spray will keep the plastic wrap from sticking to the loaves when it is removed.)

Allow dough to rise at room temperature until almost doubled, 20–40 minutes. (The amount of time depends upon the temperature of the dough and the temperature of your kitchen.) Preheat oven to 400°F.

When the dough has risen, carefully peel off the plastic wrap. Using a sharp knife, slice 5 diagonal

lines, about ½ inch deep, into the top of each baguette. (Don't worry if some of the cheese or walnuts become exposed.) Using a spray bottle filled with potable water, spray loaves until they are quite damp all over, then put the baguettes in the oven. Spray water into oven a couple of times before closing the door.

Bake baguettes for 25–35 minutes, until they are dark golden brown. Turn the baking sheet 180 degrees after 15 minutes to check on the overall color. If loaves have large light sections on the crust, bake them until you get a more even color. If they are almost all brown and are starting to get very dark brown in a few places, leave them in the oven for only a few more minutes. (Don't be afraid of a darker color. Darker crust gives much better flavor and texture. It can be rather disappointing, after all the effort, to end up with a pale bread with no character because you were nervous to overbake it and pulled it early.)

Remove baguettes from oven and baking sheet. Allow to cool a few minutes, then slice and serve bread with fresh honey and sliced ripe pears. (The bread is best eaten the same day it is baked, but you can hold it one day, wrap it in aluminum foil, and reheat it in a 375°F oven for 8–10 minutes.)

LEMON HONEY POUND CAKE

(MAKES 1 LOAF)

¾ stick (6 tablespoons) unsalted butter, softened

1½ cups all-purpose flour

¾ cup sugar

¼ teaspoon baking powder

½ teaspoon kosher salt

Juice and zest of 2 lemons, separated

¼ cup plus 1 tablespoon milk

1 large egg plus 1 egg yolk

½ teaspoon pure vanilla

¼ cup honey

½ cup water

Preheat oven to 315°F. Place butter in a large bowl. Using a rubber spatula, mix in flour, sugar, baking powder, salt, and lemon zest until lump free. (Don't overdo the mixing; mixture should be blended completely but not aerated. It should be a smooth paste that is a little thicker than peanut butter.)

In a medium bowl, whisk together milk, eggs, and vanilla. Using a rubber spatula, add milk mixture to flour mixture, working it gently into the batter just until smooth and homogenous in texture.

Pour batter into a 9 x 4½-inch loaf pan, well-greased with vegetable cooking spray, and bake for 1–1¼ hours, until a skewer poked in the center of the loaf comes out clean. Remove loaf pan from oven. (Don't be afraid of a darkish brown color on the top of the cake, as this caramelizing will only impart more flavor.) When pan is cool enough to handle, carefully turn loaf out onto a wire rack that has been positioned on a baking sheet.

Strain lemon juice into a medium bowl. Whisk in honey and water. Using a brush, paint this syrup onto the top and all sides of the cake while cake is still warm. (The cake should be really drenched with the syrup.)

When cake is completely cool, slice and serve. Garnish with vanilla ice cream, fresh strawberries, or mascarpone cheese, if you like. (Wrapped in plastic wrap, cake will last at least a week in the refrigerator.)

One Duval Street
Key West, FL 33040
(305) 296-4600
PIERHOUSE.COM
Maria Manso, Executive Chef

A chance sighting of a help-wanted sign in a New Orleans oyster bar window serendipitously launched nineteen-year-old Cuban-born Maria Manso on the road to her impressive culinary career. "I needed a job," she says. "I'd never shucked an oyster before, never even tasted one!" The chef at the all-male Cafe Sbaisa told her that if she could pick up the oysters in the back cooler and carry them all the way to the front of the restaurant, where the oyster bar was located, she could have the job.

"I was always a pretty strong girl," says Manso. "So I grabbed two boxes of oysters and carried them up to the bar, and he gave me the job." The chef taught her the fine art of oyster shucking, and she shucked away for three years before talking her way into the kitchen in 1983. "When I'd go back to get the oysters, I always stood and watched them cook," she says. "Sauté pans flying, handwritten tickets everywhere, screamin' and yellin'. It looked cool to me!"

As the only female in the kitchen, Manso felt she had to prove herself more. "I had to take the heat and hang with the boys to get promoted. It toughened me up a little bit," she recalls. It must have worked, because Manso went on to hone her craft in some of the most famous kitchens in the nation, including that of Chef Dick Brenan Jr. in New Orleans and Chef Norman Van Aken in Miami.

She moved on to hold executive chef positions at several prestigious hotels, including the Delano in Miami. But finally ready for a slower pace, she moved to Key

West in 2010, as executive chef at Bagatelle. "It was almost like coming home," she says. "I was born only 90 miles away."

Manso credits Norman Van Aken with inspiring her signature culinary concepts and visions, which she implements in her new position as executive chef at One Duval at the Pier House Resort. "He inspired me to take ingredients from all different cultures and make them work together on one plate." The Pier House, a Key West icon for forty years, sits astride the Gulf of Mexico, with sweeping water views. One can imagine that Chef Manso can almost see Cuba from her kitchen!

SAUTÉED GULF SHRIMP WITH SMOKED BACON & CREMINI MUSHROOM BEURRE BLANC

(SERVES 6)

For the beurre blanc:

1 teaspoon olive oil

6–8 cremini mushrooms, cut in half

4 slices raw smoked bacon, diced

2 medium shallots, finely chopped

1 clove garlic, finely chopped

1 cup white wine

¼ cup lemon juice

1 tablespoon heavy cream

½ teaspoon salt

¼ teaspoon freshly ground black pepper

12 tablespoons (1½ sticks) cold salted butter, cut into small cubes

For the shrimp:

2 tablespoons canola oil

36 (U-12) jumbo gulf shrimp, peeled and deveined

3 cups steamed white or jasmine rice

3 slices crispy cooked bacon, crumbled

1 bunch chives

To make the beurre blanc: Place olive oil in a small skillet over medium-high heat. Add mushrooms and sauté until softened and liquid has evaporated. Set aside.

Place a heavy medium saucepan over high heat. Add raw bacon, shallots, and garlic and cook until bacon is golden brown. Add wine and lemon juice and boil, stirring occasionally, until mixture starts to thicken, about 10–15 minutes. Reduce heat to very low and whisk in cream, sautéed mushrooms, salt, and pepper. Whisk in butter, a few cubes at a time. When butter is fully combined and the mixture is emulsified, remove from heat. (Serve immediately or store in a thermos until you are ready to serve.)

To prepare the shrimp: Place canola oil in a large skillet over high heat. Add the shrimp and sauté, stirring constantly, until pink and just cooked through. (Be careful not to overcook.) Remove from heat. Add beurre blanc sauce to the pan and toss with shrimp until they are well coated with sauce.

To serve: Place ½ cup rice in the center of each of 6 dinner plates. Arrange 6 shrimp around rice on each plate. Drizzle remaining sauce atop shrimp. Garnish each portion with a sprinkle of crispy bacon and a few chive sprigs.

CRAB & AVOCADO TIMBALE

(SERVES 4)

For the avocado mixture:

2 Hass avocados, skinned, seed removed, and
　　cut into small dice
Juice of 1 lime
1 tablespoon snipped fresh cilantro
Tabasco sauce
Salt and freshly ground black pepper

For the crab mixture:

6 ounces jumbo lump crabmeat
1 tablespoon mayonnaise
Salt and freshly ground black pepper

For the mango coulis:

1 large ripe mango, peeled and seeded
1 teaspoon rice wine vinegar
1 tablespoon extra-virgin olive oil
Salt and freshly ground black pepper

For the garnishes:

4 steamed or grilled peeled jumbo shrimp
8 cherry tomatoes
½ bunch chives

To prepare the avocado mixture: Mix avocado, lime juice, and cilantro in a medium bowl. Season with Tabasco sauce, salt, and pepper to taste. Cover bowl and refrigerate mixture until needed.

To prepare the crab mixture: Place crabmeat and mayonnaise in a medium bowl and gently mix together. Season with salt and pepper to taste.

To make the mango coulis: Puree mango in a food processor or blender. Add vinegar and oil and pulse until smooth. Season with salt and pepper to taste.

To assemble the timbales: Place four 2½-inch ring molds or cookie cutters (at least 2 inches high) on a shallow tray or baking sheet. Divide half the avocado mixture evenly among the ring molds, pressing it firmly in the ring mold with the back of a spoon. Spoon one-quarter of the crab mixture into each ring mold, pressing lightly with the back of a spoon to form an even layer. Place one-quarter of the remaining avocado mixture into each ring mold and press into an even layer. Cover with cling wrap and refrigerate for at least 1 hour.

To plate and serve: Spoon a circle of mango coulis in the center of each of 4 appetizer plates. Place a timbale ring mold on top of each and unmold timbale. Top each timbale with a shrimp. Garnish each plate with 2 cherry tomatoes and about 2 snipped chives.

PRIME 951 STEAKHOUSE

951 CAROLINE STREET
KEY WEST, FL 33040
(305) 296-4000
PRIMEKEYWEST.COM
KIM QUACH, EXECUTIVE CHEF

"I always wanted to live on an island as a kid," says Kim Quach, describing why he was drawn to Key West. "I came in 2005 to open Monty's, which is now Prime's casual sister restaurant, Dante's."

Born in Ho Chi Minh City, Vietnam, Quach immigrated to Florida with his family when he was a child. His personal journey with food began in his Orlando home, where cooking had always been a focus. "Growing up, my parents had a garden in the backyard with all the fresh produce and herbs you can imagine," he remembers. "While my brothers or sisters were playing or doing homework, I gravitated to the kitchen. Some of my fondest memories are mincing lemongrass and peppers with my mom."

After college, Quach cooked in his uncle's Chinese restaurant for a couple of years and then started at Monty's in Atlanta. "I never went to culinary school, but I was

fortunate enough to learn hands-on techniques of cooking from two chefs while I lived in Atlanta that helped develop my cooking skills," Quach says. "But Prime Steakhouse is when I really was able to get creative with my cooking."

Overlooking Conch Harbor Marina, Prime is primarily a traditional steak house, but the restaurant's owners, Dale Darmante and Mike Gilvary, themselves fishermen, ensure that an array of fresh seafood offerings come straight from the docks. "The combination of quality meats cut to our specifications, our own blend of seasonings, and the infrared broiler creates a wow factor for steak lovers," says Quach. "And nothing can beat the sweetness of fish fresh off the boat!"

"Experimenting is the best part of my profession," professes Quach. "I start with what may sound like a crazy idea to others, and through trial and error develop it into a composed dish. When a dish comes together, I think to myself, 'Wow, it worked!'"

DOUBLE BONE PORK CHOP WITH MUSHROOM CABERNET SAUCE

(SERVES 1)

For the pork chops:

1 (16-ounce) double bone, thick-cut pork chop
1 tablespoon butter, melted
Salt and freshly ground black pepper

For the mushroom cabernet sauce:

2 tablespoons butter
2 ounces button mushrooms, cleaned and sliced
Salt and freshly ground black pepper
1 cup Cabernet wine
1 tablespoon pork base*

To prepare the pork chops: Preheat oven to 375°F. Brush both sides of the pork chop with melted butter and season with salt and pepper to taste. Sear both sides of chop on a hot grill until golden brown. Transfer chop to an ovenproof skillet and finish it in the oven for 20 minutes. Remove chop to a dinner plate. Hood plate with aluminum foil to keep it warm.

To make the sauce: Place butter in the skillet over medium heat. (Do not remove any of the remaining pork bits; they will enhance the flavor of the sauce.) When butter has melted, add mushrooms and a pinch of salt and pepper. Sauté, stirring occasionally, until mushrooms begin to sweat. Stir in wine and pork base. Cook, stirring constantly, until base dissolves and wine reduces by half.

To serve: Remove tented aluminum foil from dinner plate. Pour mushroom Cabernet sauce over pork chop and serve immediately.

*Pork base is available at specialty markets and online.

ROOF TOP CAFE

308 FRONT STREET
KEY WEST, FL 33040
(305) 294-2042
ROOFTOPCAFEKEYWEST.COM
BRENDAN ORR, EXECUTIVE CHEF

Supping at the Roof Top Cafe—nestled amidst the branches of a giant mahogany tree, high above the bustle of Front Street—is like dining in an elegant tree house. So, perhaps it is fitting that the restaurant's talented executive chef first majored in forestry before forging his culinary career.

Cooking, for Brendan Orr, at first was just a means to pay his college expenses at University of Florida in Gainesville. Realizing that he enjoyed his part-time job more than his studies, Orr instead enrolled in a two-year, hands-on apprenticeship program at the American Culinary Federation in Jacksonville. He worked his way up restaurant lines for several years after graduation, before "chasing a girl" to Paris and immersing himself in the French culinary scene for four years.

Orr found the Parisian transition difficult at first. "Everything was different," he says, But with the help of an Algerian dishwasher and a couple of waiters, Orr mastered the language and everything fell into place. "I would go to the markets at four o'clock in the morning and pick out the ingredients I wanted for the day," he says. Then he would go home and go back to bed, and everything would be delivered to the restaurant by 8:00 a.m. "We used what we had, and when it was gone, it was gone," he adds. "It was a pretty nice way to live."

With several French master chef classes under his belt, Orr returned to the States in 1998 and brought his considerable talents to Louie's Backyard in Key West, where he was sous chef under Doug Shook, the man Orr considers his mentor. "Doug Shook is a phenomenal guy," praises Orr. "Talented, talented, talented!" He goes on, "He taught me some of the best rules about how to behave, because I worked for a lot of pricks in Europe—the plate throwers, the screamers. He taught me a lot about how to succeed in management without being a jerk!"

Joining Roof Top Cafe as executive chef several years ago, Orr changed the cuisine to be more seasonal, more local, more updated and modern. He describes his cuisine as locally inspired, with French techniques and Caribbean influences. Open-air and casual during the day, the restaurant is transformed in the evening, with linen, crystal and candles, twinkling tree lights, and starlight.

"Everything has to pass muster with me, obviously," Orr says when describing his kitchen, "but I have a super-talented crew here." And Orr clearly enjoys the creative process of devising new dishes, winning awards in the Key West Master Chef's Classic many years in a row. "It's a labor of love," he says of his culinary career.

DUCK TOSTADOS

(SERVES 4)

For the duck:

2 tablespoons plus 1 teaspoon kosher salt
2 tablespoons snipped fresh parsley
2 tablespoons snipped fresh sage
2 tablespoons snipped fresh thyme
1 clove garlic, thinly sliced
4 duck legs/thighs, skin removed
4¼ cups melted duck fat

For the green chili sauce:

2 poblano chilies
1 pound tomatillos, husks removed
1 clove garlic, peeled
2 jalapeños, seeded
1 cup chicken stock
½ bunch cilantro

For the tortillas and assembly:

6 (6-inch) corn tortillas
Canola, peanut, or corn oil for frying
4 ounces crème fraîche
1 cup chiffonade-snipped arugula

To prepare the duck: Mix salt with parsley, sage, thyme, and garlic. Rub seasoning mixture over all surfaces of duck legs and thighs. Place in a covered container and allow duck to cure in the refrigerator for 5 hours.

Preheat oven to 275°F. Place melted duck fat in a deep roasting pan. Brush residual salt mixture off duck legs and thighs and place them in pan. Braise duck until tender, about 2½ hours. Remove duck from fat and transfer to a paper-towel-lined plate. Allow duck to cool. Remove the cooked meat from the bones and shred. Set aside until needed. (To reheat the duck: Preheat oven to 200°F. Place duck in a covered baking pan and reheat in oven for about 20 minutes.)

To make the green chili sauce: Preheat oven to 350°F. Place poblano chilies, tomatillos, garlic, and jalapeños in a baking pan. Roast until very dark and bubbling, but not scorched. Remove from oven. When cool, peel and seed chilies. Place roasted chilies, tomatillos, garlic, and jalapeños in a blender. Add chicken stock and cilantro. Process until smooth. Set aside until needed.

For the tortillas: Cut two 3-inch rounds from each tortilla. Place a shallow layer of oil in a large skillet over medium heat. Fry tortilla rounds, turning once, until crispy. Remove with a slotted spoon and drain on paper towels.

To assemble and serve: Arrange 3 crisp tortilla rounds on a plate. Top each with a portion of warm duck, a drizzle of green chili sauce, a dollop of crème fraîche, and a sprinkling of snipped arugula.

Seared Sea Scallops with Edamame, Roasted Shiitakes & Sherry Miso Butter

(SERVES 4)

For the miso butter:

2 large shallots, diced
1 cup dry sherry
⅓ cup white miso paste
2 sticks whole butter, softened

For the edamame and shiitakes:

1 cup shelled edamame (mukimame)
2 cups shiitake mushroom caps
2 tablespoons sesame oil
2 tablespoons soy sauce
2 tablespoons sambal oelek (Asian chili sauce)

For the rice:

1½ cups basmati rice, rinsed until water runs clear
3 cups water
1 ounce soy sauce
1 tablespoon sesame oil
2 tablespoons black sesame seeds

For the scallops:

1 pound dry diver scallops
Salt and freshly ground black pepper
Flour
Clarified butter or canola oil

To make the miso butter: Place shallots, sherry, and white miso paste in a medium saucepan over medium heat. Reduce mixture by half. Stir in butter, a small portion at a time, until melted and combined with other ingredients. Set aside until needed.

To prepare the edamame and shiitakes: Place a medium saucepan of salted water over high heat. Add edamame and cook until tender, about 4 minutes. Drain edamame and plunge them into an ice bath. Drain again and set aside. (To reheat edamame for serving: Place edamame in a skillet with a little miso butter and warm them gently over low heat.)

Preheat oven to 350°F. Place raw shiitakes in a medium bowl. Add sesame oil, soy sauce, and sambal oelek and toss to combine. Transfer mixture to a baking pan and roast for about 5 minutes, taking care not to dry out the shiitakes. Remove from oven and reserve until needed.

To prepare the rice: Place rice, water, soy sauce, and sesame oil in a large saucepan over medium-high heat. Bring to a boil. Cover pan and turn off burner. After 5 minutes, fluff rice with a fork. Add sesame seeds and fluff rice again.

To prepare the scallops: Season scallops with salt and pepper. Dredge each lightly in flour. Place clarified butter or oil in a large skillet so that it coats the bottom of the pan. Place skillet over high heat. Add scallops and sear one side for 90 seconds. Turn off burner, flip scallops, cook for 10 seconds more, then remove scallops to a plate and allow them to rest.

To plate and serve: Divide rice into 4 equal servings, placing a mound in the center of each plate. Scatter cooked edamame around rice. Evenly divide the shiitakes among the 4 plates, placing them atop the rice. Top each portion with an equal amount of scallops, caramelized side up. Place a dollop of miso butter atop each scallop.

Santiago's Bodega

207 Petronia Street
Key West, FL 33040
(305) 296-7691
SANTIAGOSBODEGA.COM
Jason Dugan, Owner
José Hernandez, Executive Chef

In 2004 Jason Dugan and four friends from Kansas City packed a U-haul, headed for Key West, and along the way did an Internet search for a restaurant to buy. They hit pay dirt, gutted the place, and together rebuilt the restaurant from the ground up—hand-stained floors, tabletops, and banquettes, even the stained glass doors and the artwork.

Next came the cuisine concept. Dugan found tapas intriguing because it was "all about coming together with a group of people you enjoy, dining on food with different flavor profiles, and sharing it family style." "After deciding on the tapas concept," says Dugan, "I began looking through books for a name. On my end table were two books I had recently read: *The Old Man and the Sea* and *The Alchemist*. The main character in both books have the same name—Santiago. It was fate or serendipity, whichever or both."

In Spanish, *a bodega* means "a little shop," often hidden around the corner in a residential neighborhood. Santiago's Bodega is a little gem of a restaurant "hidden" on a quiet side street, three blocks off bustling Duval. It was the first place executive chef José Hernandez put in an application when he came to Key West two days before Christmas in 2008. "I didn't think anything of it," he recalls, referring to his brief interview with Dugan.

"But I didn't even get around the corner before I got a call from him," he laughs, "saying, 'Can you start tonight?'"

Hernandez, born in Key West but raised since age seven in Washington State, attended culinary school at the local community college. But he credits the chef at the Steelhead in Spokane, where he worked in his mid-twenties, with teaching him French techniques, flavor combinations, and the science behind the food. "He didn't take 'no' or 'sorry' for an answer," states Hernandez. "He made me do the job until it was done right. Because of that, it made me stronger as a chef and as a person."

The tapas at Santiago's are flavor explosions from a variety of cuisines—French, Mediterranean, Asian, Greek, and, of course, Spanish. "The challenge is taking big classic meals and making them into a combination of little 'wow' bites," says Hernandez. "We all bring a little something different to the table," he says, referring to his culinary team. "On any given night you can be eating food from anywhere."

"When I'm not here," says Hernandez, "I'm home researching food—what's happening in New York, San Francisco, Italy. I don't know what I would do with myself if I had to leave the kitchen!"

Yellowfin Tuna Ceviche

(SERVES 4)

For the ceviche:

2 tomatoes
2 jalapeños
1 tablespoon olive oil
Salt and freshly ground black pepper
2 pounds yellowfin tuna loin, cut into 24 (1-inch) cubes
1 red onion, cut into ½-inch dice
1 cup key lime juice
1 cup orange juice
½ cup tomato juice
1 teaspoon Tabasco sauce
1 teaspoon sugar

For plating and serving:

2 avocados, peeled, seeded, and each
   cut into 12 large cubes
1 large mango, peeled, seeded, and
   cut into 24 (½-inch) cubes
Fresh cilantro leaves

To prepare the ceviche: Preheat oven to 375°F. Place tomatoes and jalapeños in a shallow baking dish, drizzle with olive oil, and season with salt and pepper to taste. Roast for 20–30 minutes.

Allow tomatoes and jalapeños to cool, then peel, seed, and finely dice them. Place them in a large covered container and add tuna cubes and onions. Mix juices, Tabasco, sugar, and 1 teaspoon salt in a medium bowl. Pour marinade over tuna mixture and toss to mix. Cover and refrigerate at least 2 hours or up to 36 hours.

To plate and serve: For each serving, place 6 cubes of avocado, 6 cubes of mango, 6 pieces of tuna, and ¼ cup ceviche marinade (with vegetables) in an individual bowl. Toss to mix. Garnish with a sprinkle of cilantro leaves.

Korean-Style Short Ribs with Cherry-Hoisin Glaze & Orange-Miso Slaw

(SERVES 10)

For the short ribs:

10 pounds beef short-rib racks
4 (32-ounce) cartons beef stock
Vegetable oil for frying
Cornstarch

For the cherry-hoisin glaze:

2 ounces fermented black beans
1 cup soy sauce
8 ounces frozen tart cherries
3 tablespoons molasses
1 tablespoon rice wine vinegar
¼ cup minced garlic
1 tablespoon sesame oil
⅛ teaspoon freshly ground black pepper
1 tablespoon Sriracha
1 cup brown sugar
Pinch of Chinese Five Spice powder
2 cups sweet chili sauce

For the orange-miso vinaigrette:

3 tablespoons miso paste
¾ cup fresh orange juice
Zest of 1 orange
¾ cup rice wine vinegar
4 tablespoons sugar
¼ teaspoon freshly ground black pepper
½ teaspoon salt
2 tablespoons sesame oil
1¼ cup vegetable oil

For the slaw:

½ red cabbage, chopped in food processor
½ red onion, sliced very thin
1 carrot, peeled and grated

½ red bell pepper, cut in julienne
¼ cup snipped cilantro leaves, divided
¾ cup orange-miso vinaigrette

To prepare the short ribs: Preheat oven to 350°F. Place ribs and beef stock in a large covered ovenproof pot and braise for 3 hours. Remove from cooking liquid and cut into individual ribs between the bones. Refrigerate ribs in a covered container for at least 2 hours.

To make the glaze: Place all the ingredients in a food processor and process until smooth. Transfer to a covered container and refrigerate until needed.

To make the vinaigrette: Place all the ingredients except the oils in a blender and process until smooth. Slowly blend in sesame oil and vegetable oil until emulsified. Transfer to a covered container and refrigerate until needed.

To prepare the orange-miso slaw: Place cabbage, onions, carrots, bell peppers, and 3 tablespoons snipped cilantro in a large covered container. Toss with 6 ounces orange miso vinaigrette, cover, and refrigerate until needed.

To plate and serve: Heat manufacturer's recommended amount of oil in a deep-fat fryer to 350°F. Dust short ribs with cornstarch. Deep-fry ribs for 5 minutes and drain on paper towels. Transfer ribs to a large bowl and toss with cherry-hoisin glaze. Place a nest of orange-miso slaw in the center of each individual plate. Place about a pound of ribs atop slaw. Sprinkle with remaining snipped cilantro leaves.

SQUARE ONE

1075 DUVAL STREET
KEY WEST, FL 33040
(305) 296-4300
SQUAREONEKEYWEST.COM
DOMINIQUE FALKNER, CAROLYN SULLIVAN, AND CARMELO VITALE,
OWNERS; LEA FETTIS, EXECUTIVE CHEF; DENISE LEARY, PASTRY CHEF

"I love food," says Carolyn Sullivan, who owns Square One with Carmelo Vitale and Dominique Falkner. "It is in my blood!" Sullivan and Vitale owned the popular La Trattoria Italian restaurant for nineteen years, and with Carmelo's brother Constantino, they also own the Bottle Cap Groove Lounge, a local dance-club favorite. They teamed up with Falkner, who also owns Banana Cafe, in 2013 to purchase another perennial Key West favorite, Square One.

The trio created a hipper, sleeker, more metropolitan decor in the restaurant's interior and updated the cuisine to reflect their joint philosophy of New American Table. "America is a melting pot," says Sullivan, "so incorporating essences of other countries' cuisines gives the chef an open playing field to be more creative."

English-born executive chef Lea Fettis is just that . . . creative. A veritable fixture in many Key West kitchens since he washed ashore in 1995 from Devon, Fettis follows a personal formula for creating new dishes: "I try to think of three or four really bazooka-flavored foods, foods that taste amazing, and then figure out how they can work together," he says. "I don't overwork a dish. I never use more than four components on a plate." Fettis feels it is important to use flavors that people love and then make sure to use semantics on the menu that convey the food to diners in layman's language they can understand.

Pastry chef Denise Leary, a New England native, spent twenty-eight years at Key West's Roof Top Cafe honing her craft. She credits the former owner's mother, Katherine Smith, with discovering that Leary had a knack for baking and then teaching her that fine art. When creating Pirate's Pie, says Leary, "I wanted to do something different with key lime pie, so I played with the chocolate/cherry combination." She continues, "If I don't make Pirate's Pie as a dessert special, the waitstaff is not happy because it is such a big seller."

Square One's staff—both front and back of the house—operates like a well-oiled family team (Sullivan and Vitale's son Oliver is a server). "Everyone really cares about every single aspect of the diner's experience at Square One," Sullivan says. "Here we truly care."

SHRIMP & GRITS

(SERVES 4)

For the sauce:

4 ounces pancetta or bacon, cut in small dice
2 ears sweet corn
1 small roasted red pepper, diced
1 tablespoon chopped fresh cilantro
¼ teaspoon cayenne pepper
1 teaspoon ground cumin
½ bunch scallions, chopped
2 cups heavy cream
2 sticks unsalted butter, cut into ½-inch pieces
Salt and freshly ground black pepper

For the grits:

3 cups chicken broth
1 cup instant grits
4 tablespoons butter
4 ounces Fontina cheese, grated

For the shrimp:

20 large Key West pink shrimp, peeled and deveined
Salt and freshly ground black pepper
½ cup clarified butter

Handful of cilantro leaves

To make the sauce: Place a medium saucepan over medium-low heat. Add pancetta to pan and stir until fat has rendered. Cut corn kernels off cob and add them to pancetta. Cook mixture over medium heat, stirring frequently, until it starts to brown. Add red pepper, cilantro, cayenne, cumin, and scallions and cook for 1 minute. Add cream and bring to a boil, stirring frequently. (Watch carefully, as the cream will rise over the edge of the saucepan.)

As soon as cream starts to boil, reduce heat to medium-low. Reduce cream by half, stirring occasionally. Whisk in butter, a few pieces at a time, until all is incorporated into the sauce. Season with salt and pepper to taste. Remove sauce from heat, cover, and keep it in a warm place. (Do not leave on the stove; sauce will break.)

To prepare the grits: Place broth in a medium saucepan over medium heat. Bring to a boil, then slowly whisk in the grits. Reduce heat to medium-low and cook grits for about 6 minutes, stirring occasionally. (If grits get too thick, add a little more broth.) Stir in butter and Fontina. Remove grits from heat, cover, and keep them in a warm place on the stove.

To prepare the shrimp: Set a cast-iron grill pan on an outdoor barbecue grill or on the stove over high heat. Season shrimp with salt and pepper and dip them in clarified butter. Shake off the excess butter and place shrimp on the hot grill pan. Cook shrimp for about 2 minutes. Turn them over and cook 1 minute more, until they are no longer translucent in the center. Remove shrimp from heat.

To plate and serve: Place a cup-size portion of grits on each of 4 dinner plates. Arrange 5 shrimp atop each portion of grits. Spoon sauce over shrimp and garnish with a sprinkling of cilantro leaves.

PIRATE'S PIE

(MAKES 1 PIE)

For the crust:

2¼ cups Oreo cookie crumbs
¼ cup clarified butter
⅛ teaspoon salt
1 teaspoon unsalted butter

For the key lime layer:

3 large egg yolks
1 (14-ounce) can sweetened condensed milk
5½ ounces bottled key lime juice

For the cherry-chocolate layer:

3 ounces dark chocolate
1 tablespoon unsalted butter
¼ cup heavy cream
¾ cup dark, sweet canned cherries, drained

For the meringue:

8 large egg whites
⅛ teaspoon cream of tartar
½ cup granulated sugar
1 teaspoon cocoa powder

To prepare the crust: Preheat oven to 350°F. Mix Oreo crumbs, clarified butter, and salt in a medium bowl. Pat crumb mixture into a 9-inch pie plate that has been greased with unsalted butter. Bake for 5 minutes. Remove from oven and allow crust to cool.

To prepare the key lime layer: Beat egg yolks in the large bowl of an electric mixer. Add sweetened condensed milk and mix until well combined. With mixer at slow speed, slowly add key lime juice. When smooth, pour filling into cooled crust. Bake for 5 minutes. Remove pie from oven and allow it to rest for 10 minutes.

To prepare the cherry-chocolate layer: Melt chocolate, butter, and cream in a double boiler over low heat. Remove from heat and allow mixture to cool slightly. Stir in the cherries. Spread chocolate-cherry mixture on top of key lime pie filling.

To prepare the meringue: Beat egg whites and cream of tartar in the large bowl of an electric mixer on high speed until egg whites begin to foam. Continuing at high speed, slowly beat in sugar until stiff peaks form. Swirl meringue on top of pie. Place cocoa powder in a sifter and sprinkle powder over the meringue-topped pie. With a rubber spatula, lightly swirl the cocoa powder into the meringue. Bake for 8–10 minutes or until meringue is light brown.

Chef Ben, Ziggie & Mad Dog's: "I always tell people to use a recipe just as a guide. The recipe is not cooking the food, you are! Practice makes perfect, and some mistakes are the best learning tools when it comes to food. I guarantee that every chef will have a great dish born from a mistake."

Pastry Chef Denise, Square One: "When baking, follow the recipe closely for chemical things like eggs, baking powder, and baking soda, but you can improvise with other ingredients. And always use large eggs when baking."

Chef Lynn, Square Grouper: "Don't be afraid to experiment. That's how everything is created."

Chef Doug, Louie's Backyard: "Use a sharp knife and a hot pan. Pay attention. You can't cook in an offhand way."

Chef Todd, Latitudes: "Learn the fundamentals: braise, sauté, sear, grill. Don't use the microwave. Salt is a flavor enhancer; it is not for saltiness. Get sea salt; it makes a huge difference."

Chef Jouvens, Pierre's: "Develop a flavor memory, because you've got to trust taste. Taste the food as you go along. Have fun with cooking. A recipe is just a guideline. Be adventurous. Substitute ingredients."

Chef Luigi, Morada Bay: "Balance colors, flavors, and textures on a plate. And use a sharp knife."

Chef Martin, Martin's Restaurant: "Make the dish, then add salt to taste. You can always add. You can never take back."

Chef Jason, Santiago's Bodega: "Get out of your comfort zone. Don't use a recipe as a definition, but use it as a guideline. Taste everything and season throughout every step."

Chef Dani, Better Than Sex: "If something doesn't work the first time, don't throw it away. Make it into something else, like bread pudding. Bread pudding is one of the most versatile and forgiving recipes that there is out there."

Chef Brendan, Roof Top Cafe: "Salt doesn't have to be your enemy. Season appropriately. (If you salt pasta water before cooking, you'll never have to salt the pasta afterward.) Use lots of fresh acids as seasonings—citrus juice, citrus zest, good-quality vinegars. These fool your brain into the perception that you're getting the correct seasoning without it being too salty."

Chef Darren, Nine One Five: "Keep it simple and taste as you go along. And use a good olive oil and a good vinegar."

Chef Peter, Fish House Encore: "Don't use too many herbs and spices together. Less is always more."

Chef Richard, Atlantic's Edge: "Don't take cooking too seriously. It's fun!"

Chef Dominique, Banana Cafe: "Seafood is delicate. The less it is 'handled,' the better. Fresh fish and seafood should have no odor at all. The flesh of the fish should be firm with no elasticity."

STRIP HOUSE KEY WEST

THE REACH RESORT
1435 SIMONTON STREET
KEY WEST, FL 33040
(305) 295-9669
STRIPHOUSEKEYWEST.COM
BILL ZUCOSKY, EXECUTIVE CHEF

"I got my culinary start later in life," says Bill Zucosky, executive chef of Strip House Key West. "By trade I was a flooring installer. I've always loved cooking and found myself in the kitchen constantly. One day I just decided to put down my carpet knife and pick up a chef's knife, and I've never looked back."

While attending the New York Restaurant School in Manhattan, Zucosky worked at two four-star NYC restaurants, La Caravelle and Chanterelle. "I basically worked in a closet peeling carrots and onions, cleaning lobsters, and doing grunt work," he says, "but I was a part of something spectacular, and I loved it!"

After culinary school, Zucosky cooked for three years at the Frog and the Peach, the top restaurant in New Jersey. "That is where I learned and forged my culinary skills and my love for the kitchen," he says. "I was exposed to the finer things in life, and I was just one big sponge." Joining Strip House was a natural. "I've always loved cooking over an open fire," says Zucosky. "I was a Boy Scout as a kid and loved camping. Working in a steak house is the closest I can get to that."

As executive chef of both Strip House Key West and Strip House New Jersey, and based in New Jersey three weeks out of each month, Zucosky relies on executive sous chef Christopher Dennis and sous chefs Jeffrey Lane and Hurshel Cawvey to keep the wheels turning and the fires burning at the Key West steak house. "They are a great group of men, and we're lucky to have them at Strip House," says Zucosky.

Strip House is located in the Reach Resort on the shores of the Atlantic. "It is situated on a beautiful white sand beach," says Zucosky. "We have gorgeous al fresco dining with a spectacular view. Our restaurant is dark, quiet, and romantic."

For "the perfect steak," Zucosky recommends a strip steak because it has intense marbling without the excess fat. "If you prefer a leaner cut, then go with a filet mignon, and if the opposite is what you like, then by all means go with a rib chop," he says. He likes coating the steak with safflower oil because the oil's high smoking point aids the char without burning. "Please do not use olive oil!" he advises.

A high temperature is very important when grilling because the intense heat causes the "char" that caramelizes and crusts the steak. And the Strip House secret to the perfect steak? "At Strip House we finish all of our steaks with coarse sea salt and clarified butter," Zucosky divulges.

THE PERFECT STEAK

(SERVES 4)

2 (1½-inch-thick) center-cut strip steaks
2 tablespoons safflower oil
Kosher salt
Freshly ground black pepper
½ teaspoon coarse sea salt
1 tablespoon clarified butter

Remove steaks from refrigerator 30 minutes prior to cooking. Turn gas grill to highest setting and preheat for 10 minutes or build a very hot charcoal fire. (The grill is hot enough when you can hold your hand over it for only 2–3 seconds.)

Wipe steaks with paper towels to remove any excess blood or moisture from the surface. Remove silver skin and any excess fat with a sharp knife. Coat both sides of steaks with safflower oil. Season steaks liberally with kosher salt and freshly ground black pepper. (Some of the salt and pepper will fall off during the cooking process.)

Place steaks on hot grill and cook with lid open for 4–6 minutes. (If flame flares up, move the steak to the other side of the grill. Move steaks as necessary to avoid flare-ups.) Flip steaks when undersides have a beautiful, dark chestnut brown char on them. Cook another 4–6 minutes for medium-rare and remove from heat.

Allow steaks to rest for 5 minutes. (Resting allows juices to redistribute throughout the steak. If you cut the steak too soon, all the juices will be lost.) Slice steaks ½ inch thick. Divide slices among 4 dinner plates. Season steak slices with a sprinkling of sea salt and drizzle with clarified butter. Serve immediately with Truffle Creamed Spinach.

Truffle Creamed Spinach

(SERVES 4)

1 teaspoon salt
1 pound fresh baby spinach
1½ tablespoons extra-virgin olive oil
¼ cup minced shallots
1½ cups heavy cream
⅓ cup black truffle butter
½ cup grated Parmesan cheese
1 tablespoon white truffle oil
Salt and freshly ground black pepper to taste

Place 1 teaspoon salt in a pot of water and bring to a boil over high heat. Quickly blanch spinach, drain it, and immediately transfer it to an ice bath to cool it down. When spinach is cool, remove it from the ice bath and squeeze out all the water. (Make sure the spinach is as dry as possible or the creamed spinach will be watery.) Chop squeezed spinach into ½-inch pieces with a sharp knife.

Add olive oil to a nonreactive soup pot over medium heat. When oil is hot, add shallots and sauté until translucent, making sure not to brown them. Add heavy cream, all at once, and bring to a simmer. Whisk in truffle butter and then fold in chopped spinach. Bring to a simmer and cook for 10 minutes, stirring occasionally. Reduce heat to low and stir in Parmesan cheese and white truffle oil. Season with salt and pepper to taste and serve immediately.

Tip: Chef Bill recommends using D'Artagnan Black Truffle Butter. It and white truffle oil can be purchased online or in a gourmet food store.

Director of Operations/Executive Chef, Pat Croce & Co. Key West Group

Michael Schultz's first foray into cooking was literally a trial by fire. Bussing tables at the Lobster House in Cape May, New Jersey, at age fifteen, he was thrown into the kitchen as the fry guy suddenly one night to man a six-bank fry station. "I had never even turned on a stove before," he remembers. "It was awesome," he says. "I was hooked." But not until, inexperience showing, he set the grease trap on fire, burning off his eyebrows, eyelashes, and all the hair on his arms!

But as the old saying goes, "He's come a long way, baby," and what a culinary journey it has been. After mustering out of the navy when he shattered his hip jumping out of a helicopter, Schultz followed his first love, cooking, to the kitchen of a Michelin-quality restaurant opening up in Philadelphia. "I was a sponge," says Schultz. "I went in early every day."

The biggest influence on his career was a stint in George Perrier's kitchen at Le Bec Fin. "It was brutal," he recalls. "The chef was tyrannical. He threw legendary tirades. He was so strict. He set high standards, but it gave you something to strive for." Here Schultz experienced working with "amazing imported ingredients" for the first time. "Everything was from scratch, no shortcuts," he says.

Schultz moved from restaurant to restaurant—Jersey shore, Philadelphia, South Carolina—honing his craft, before landing the "dream job" as executive chef to movie director/producer M. Night Shyamalan in 2002. "I prepared a twenty-one-course lunch as my tryout," he exclaims. The studio was on a working horse ranch in Pennsylvania. "The biggest stars in the world were there all the time," he says.

After eight surreal years traveling to exotic locations with the production company, Schultz—having just spent a month "cooking on an iceberg" in Greenland—decided he wanted the sun. "That's it," he decided. "I'm moving to Key West. I'm tired of the cold." Schultz hooked up with Pat Croce in 2012, when Croce put together his group of iconic Key West restaurants. "He needed a guy to oversee the food end of the restaurants," he says, which include Turtle Kraals, Half Shell Raw Bar, Green Parrot, Rum Barrel, Charlie Mac's, and Island Dogs Bar. "We are solidifying a brand for each one," Schultz states. "You get a different experience in every restaurant."

Schultz still cooks "all the time," dipping into the Croce-group restaurant kitchens, constantly menu testing and trying out new ideas with his culinary teams. His latest endeavor is the new catering division, Royal Palm Catering. Schultz has devised high-end, served-in-your-home, ten-course, themed tasting dinners such as "The Holidays," which starts with New Year's Eve and ends with Christmas, celebrating each holiday of the year, course by course. "Santa himself brings out the final course," says Schultz. "This is my creative outlet," he says. "I need that."

Turtle Kraals

231 Margaret Street
Key West, FL 33040
(305) 294-2640
TURTLEKRAALS.COM
Ricardo Hernandez Martinez, Executive Chef

Growing up on Mexico's Yucatan peninsula, Ricardo Hernandez Martinez loved cooking with his Spanish-born grandmother, who taught him about the old Mayan cuisine. Bussing tables and serving at Restaurant Leo when he was fifteen, Martinez made his way to the kitchen, where he chopped, trained, and learned, all the way up the line.

When he was twenty-four, the owner of Sandy's Cafe in Key West, who was from Martinez's hometown in Mexico, offered him a cooking job, and he jumped at the chance to immigrate to America. Martinez learned from Key West's best. After five years at Sandy's, he moved to Banana Cafe, where he credits owner Dani Dahon with teaching him French cooking techniques. From there he moved to Nine One Five and Alonzo's before landing at Turtle Kraals as executive chef. "Work in the kitchen is a challenge," says Martinez. "You never stop learning. You have a lot of responsibility and a lot of stress, too, but I like it."

Purchased by former owner of the Philadelphia 76ers and longtime Key West resident Pat Croce in 2012, Turtle Kraals sits on the site of yesteryear's turtle pens (called kraals) and docks. "The kraals were a dark period in Key West history," says Michael Schultz, Croce Group executive chef and director of operations (see sidebar). "The treatment of the turtles in those days was inhumane," he adds.

Today, however, the restaurant that is Turtle Kraals enjoys a fabulous view of the waterfront bight and shines with authentic Cuban and Caribbean cuisine. Perhaps the brightest jewel is the *cevicheria*, Schultz's brainchild. Schultz went to Peru for an intensive ten-day immersion in the fine art of ceviche and returned with a palate of fresh flavors and techniques, which he taught to his culinary staff.

Fish and seafood could not be fresher at Turtle Kraals, which shares its waterfront location with Half Shell Fish Market and sister restaurant Half Shell Raw Bar. Vessels come directly to their docks at the bight every day, selling their catch-of-the-day exclusively to the market and the two restaurants.

Turtle Kraals still features turtle races outside the restaurant on Mondays and Fridays, a tradition since the restaurant first opened in 1980. "They used to be loggerheads and greens, back in the day," states Schultz. "Now they are just little turtles, but you can still win a money prize!"

Ropa Vieja

(SERVES 4)

2 quarts (64 ounces) chicken stock plus 1 cup
¼ cup blended oil
½ cup diced green bell peppers
½ cup diced red bell peppers
½ diced white onions
½ cup tomato paste
¼ cup chopped garlic
2 tablespoons chopped fresh thyme
2 tablespoons chopped fresh oregano
1½ teaspoons ground cumin seed
2 bay leaves
2 tablespoons Sriracha
2 pounds beef brisket, trimmed of fat
½ cup diced tomatoes
Kosher salt and white pepper to taste
4 sprigs cilantro

Place chicken stock in a large saucepot over medium-high heat and bring it to a boil. Reduce heat to a simmer.

Meanwhile, heat oil in a separate large saucepot over medium heat. Add bell peppers and onions and sauté for 5 minutes, until vegetables are softened. Add tomato paste, garlic, thyme, and oregano and cook for 3 minutes, stirring frequently. Add 2 quarts chicken stock, cumin, bay leaves, and Sriracha. Stir, bring to a boil, then add brisket.

Reduce heat to medium-low. Cover pot with a lid or heavy foil. Braise the brisket for 3 hours or until very tender. You may have to add some or all of the remaining 1 cup stock as the brisket cooks. Check liquid level every 30 minutes.

When brisket is tender, carefully remove it and allow it to rest until it is cool enough to handle. Using clean hands, break the brisket apart into thin strands. (This should happen very easily.) Place shredded brisket back into the cooking liquid and reheat it. Add the diced tomatoes and season with salt and pepper to taste.

To plate and serve: Divide the ropa vieja among 4 dinner plates. Garnish with a sprig of cilantro. Serve with yellow rice and black beans.

Nikkei Ceviche

(SERVES 6)

For the grouper:

1¼ pounds red grouper

For the candied limes*:

¾ cup sugar
¾ cup water
2 Persian limes, sliced ¼ inch thick

For the marinade:

1 cup soy sauce
½ cup yuzu or fresh lemon juice
1½ tablespoons sesame oil
2 tablespoons tamarind puree
1 tablespoon agave nectar
1 cup fresh key lime juice

For the ceviche vegetables:

½ cup peeled celery hearts, sliced crosswise
⅛ inch thick
1 large (about 6 ounces) peeled sweet potato
Orange juice
1½ cups very thinly sliced red onions

For assembly:

1–1½ Thai chilies, very thinly sliced crosswise
1½ tablespoons snipped fresh Thai basil
1½ tablespoons snipped fresh mint
1½ tablespoons snipped fresh cilantro
½ cup diced candied limes, optional*
Kosher salt
Freshly popped popcorn*

One week ahead: Wrap grouper fillet in plastic wrap. Add a second layer of plastic wrap and wrap grouper tightly. Place grouper in the freezer for 1 week to kill any microorganisms.

To prepare the candied limes: Place sugar and water in a small saucepan over high heat. Bring to a boil until sugar has dissolved, forming a simple syrup. Add lime slices. Gently move the slices around in the syrup so that they cook evenly. Bring the simple syrup back to a boil on high heat, then turn off the heat. Let the limes cool in the syrup, then transfer limes and syrup to a covered container and refrigerate until needed. Remove limes from syrup with a slotted spoon before using.

To prepare the grouper: Remove grouper from freezer and allow it to thaw slightly. (The fish will be easier to clean and prepare if it is partially frozen.) Remove the collarbones along with the bloodline and discard. Keep the grouper in a stainless-steel pan on top of another pan that is filled with ice water to keep the fish very cold during preparation. Dice the grouper into ½-inch cubes and place in an airtight container with a layer of paper towels at the bottom to catch any residual moisture that occurs during the thawing process.

To make the marinade: Place all the ingredients in a blender and pulse until smooth. Transfer to a covered container and refrigerate until needed.

To prepare the ceviche vegetables: Place sliced celery in a bowl of ice water to keep it crisp. Cut the sweet potatoes into ½-inch dice. Place them in a medium saucepan with orange juice to cover by 1 inch. Cook potatoes on high heat until they are fork tender. Drain potatoes, transfer them to

a paper-towel-lined baking sheet, and refrigerate until they cool.

Rinse onions in a bowl of cool water. Drain and repeat process two more times with fresh water each time. Place onions in a covered container and refrigerate.

To assemble and serve: Drain celery. Place grouper, celery, sweet potatoes, onions, chilies, basil, mint, cilantro, and candied limes in a large stainless-steel bowl. Mix gently with a spoon. Pour marinade into the bowl and gently stir to combine. Add kosher salt to taste. (Don't add too much salt, as the soy sauce contains a lot of salt.) Mix the ceviche for 30–45 seconds, then divide it equally among 6 chilled bowls. Serve with fresh popcorn on the side.

*Chef Michael Schultz notes: "The candied limes are optional in this recipe but add a special flavor to the ceviche. Reserve the syrup for use in mojito cocktails." He adds, "Normally the Peruvians use cancha (fried corn nuts), but they are difficult to find and expensive. Popcorn balances the acidity of the ceviche beautifully."

Index

aioli, 94, 97–98, 166–67
alcoholic beverages, 119, 120, 121, 122, 123, 139, 160
almonds, 92–93, 165–66
Andouille sausage, 166–67
apples, 88–89
artichokes, 11, 166–67
Asian Raw Beef Salad, 77
asparagus, 11, 146–48, 148–49
au poivre sauce, 29–30
avocados, 56, 177, 185

bacon, 175, 189
baguettes, 171–72
barbecue sauces, 138–39
basil, 9, 70, 98
beef, 29–30, 77, 128–29, 187, 195, 199
Beef Yu-Ke, 77
beurre blanc, 34–35, 148–49
beverages, 27, 119, 120, 121, 122, 123, 139, 160
bisques, 12, 14
Blackened Scallops with Risotto-Style Israeli Couscous, 116–17
bok choy, 116–17
brassica, 34–35
bread puddings, 113–14
breads, 171–72
brownies, 153
brussels sprouts, 103
burgers, 24
Butter Poached Florida Lobster Tail with Creamy Herb Polenta, Champagne Beurre Blanc, Caviar & Asparagus, 148–49
butters, 183

cabbage, 128, 187
calamari, 71
canistel, 27
Canistel Strawberry Shake, 27
capers, 40–41

Caramelized Brussels Sprouts with Pancetta & Pecorino Romano, 103
Castaway's Wreck Diver-Style Lionfish, 76
cauliflower, 146–48, 151
Cauliflower-Chèvre Puree, 151
caviar, 148–49
celery hearts, 200–201
ceviche, 90, 185, 200–201
Champagne Beurre Blanc, 148–49
Champagne Sauerkraut, 155–56
charity events, 168–69
cheese, 31, 81–82, 103, 143, 151, 159, 162–63, 171–72
cherries, 187, 191
Cherry-Hoisin Glaze, 187
chicken, 18
chocolate, 57, 113–14, 153, 191
Chocolate Brownie Crème Brûlée, 153
Chocolate Valencia, 57
chorizo sausages, 51–52, 142, 143
chowders, 135
cilantro, 8
Cilantro-Lime Pesto, 8
clams, 162–63
Coconut Chorizo Stew Topped with Grilled Grouper, 142
cod, 34–35
conch, 82, 135
condiments, 23
cooking competitions, 168–69
corn, 52–53, 88–89, 142
couscous, 116–17
crab, 12, 49, 162–63, 166–67, 177
Crab & Avocado Timbale, 177
Crab Cakes with Fingerling Potatoes, Andouille Sausage, Artichokes & Lemon Aioli, 166–67

Creamy Herb Polenta, 148–49
crème brûlée, 153
Cremini Mushroom Beurre Blanc, 175
Cuban Mix Sandwich, 125–26
Cuban Pork Empanadas with Guava Barbecue Sauce, 138–39
custards, 113–14, 153

Dijon mustard, 155–56
dips, 21
donuts, 132–33
Dottie's Key Largo Smoked Fish Dip, 21
Double Bone Pork Chop with Mushroom Cabernet Sauce, 179
dressings, 110–11, 128
duck, 181
Duck Tostados, 181

edamame, 183
eggs, 105, 143
empanadas, 138–39
Encore Pumpkin Bisque with Crabmeat, 12

festivals, 168–69
fish, 11, 21, 48. See also specific types of fish
Fish Flagler, 11
Food and Wine Festival, 168–69
Fresh Catch-of-the-Day with Shrimp Portofino Sauce, 48
fritters, 82
Frozen Mango Mint Margarita, 121

garlic, 146
ginger, 67–68
glazes, 132–33, 187

gnocchi, 107–8
Gorgonzola-Walnut Baguettes, 171–72
green beans, 41–42, 107–8
Green Chili Sauce, 181
Green Parrot Root Beer Barrel, 122
green pea tendrils, 40–41
Grilled Lamb Rib Chops with Cauliflower-Chèvre Puree & Sun-dried Tomato Relish, 151
Grilled Octopus with Crispy Capers, Extra-Virgin Olive Oil, Smoked Paprika & Green Pea Tendrils, 40–41
grits, 51–52, 189–90
grouper, 71, 90, 92–93, 142, 146–48, 155–56, 200–201
Grouper Dijon over Champagne Sauerkraut, 155–56
Guava Barbecue Sauce, 138–39

ham, 56
hamachi, 37
haricots verts, 41–42, 107–8
Hazelnut Chicken, 18
Hazelnut Sauce, 18
Heirloom Tomato & Parsley Salad, 41–42
hogfish, 34–35, 41–42, 60
Hogfish à la Plancha, 34–35
Hogfish Tropical, 60
hollandaise sauce, 105, 155–56
Hot Tin Huevos Rancheros, 143

ice cream, 27, 113–14
Inside-Out Juicy Lucy Burger, 24
Island Pepper Aioli, 94
Island Shrimp Cakes with Island Pepper Aioli, 94

Israeli Couscous, 116–17
Italian sausage, 81–82

Ke Ke Beach Key Lime Cream Liqueur, 160
ketchup, 23
Key Lime Dressing, 110
key lime juice, 63, 64–65, 84, 85, 110–11, 191
Key Lime Martini, 160
Key Lime Parfait, 63
Key Lime Pie, Manny & Isa's, 85
Key West Pink Shrimp with Vera Cruz Sauce, 119
Korean Bulgogi Tacos, 128–29
Korean-Style Short Ribs with Cherry-Hoisin Glaze & Orange-Miso Slaw, 187

lamb, 151, 165–66
lasagna, 162–63
Lemon Aioli, 166–67
Lemon Honey Pound Cake, 173
lemons, 166–67, 173
lime, 8
limes, 110–11, 128–29
lionfish, 76, 78
Liquor 43, 123
lobster, 14–15, 31, 52–53, 74, 88–89, 148–49, 162–63
Lobster Bisque, 14–15
Lobster-Stuffed Squash Blossom Salad, 52–53
Lobster with Roasted Corn & Apple Risotto, 88–89
Local Hogfish Meunière with Olive Oil Poached Potatoes, Haricots Verts, and Heirloom Tomato & Parsley Salad, 41–42

Macadamia Nut Jerk Pesto, 98
mahi-mahi, 90

mangos, 45, 121, 177, 185
Mango Tropical Salsa, 45
Manny & Isa's Key Lime Pie, 85
MARC (Monroe Association for ReMARCable Citizens), 168–69
margaritas, 121
marinades, 40–41, 97–98, 200–201
martinis, 160
Master Chef's Classic, 168–69
M.E.A.T.'s Signature Ketchup, 23
Miso Braised Pork Belly & Key Lime-Chili Seared Sea Scallops over Risotto, 64–65
miso paste, 64–65, 183, 187
Moroccan Lamb Loin with Vegetable Tagine, 165–66
Mushroom Cabernet Sauce, 179
mushrooms, 175, 179, 183
mustard greens, baby, 34–35

Nikkei Ceviche, 200–201
nuts, 17, 92–93, 98, 165–66, 171–72

octopus, 40–41
Olive Oil Poached Potatoes, 41–42
Orange-Miso Slaw, 187
oranges, 18, 57, 187

Pacific Rim Tuna Poke, 97–98
Pan-Seared Scallops Served over Pesto Pasta, 70
parfaits, 63
Parisian Gnocchi, 107–8
Parmesan Grit Cakes, 51–52
parsley, 41–42
pasta, 8, 31, 70, 98, 107–8
Pasta with Shrimp & Cilantro-Lime Pesto, 8

pepperoni, 81–82
Perfect Steak, The, 195
pesto sauce, 8, 70, 98
pies, 85, 191
pineapple, 92–93, 132–33
Pirate's Pie, 191
Pistachio-Encrusted Yellowtail
    Snapper with Sweet Chili
    Sauce, 17
pistaschios, 17
pizza, 81–82
polenta, 148–49
Ponzu Sauce, 37
pork, 56, 64–65, 81–82,
    125–26, 138–39, 166–67,
    175, 179, 189
potatoes, 29–30, 41–42, 105,
    135, 146–48, 166–67
pound cakes, 173
prosciutto, 9, 105
puddings, bread, 113–14
pumpkin, 12
Pumpkin Bisque with
    Crabmeat, Encore, 12

Rasta Pasta with Macadamia
    Nut Jerk Pesto, 98
Red Conch Chowder, 135
relishes, 92–93, 151
rice, 64–65, 67–68, 88–89, 119,
    175, 183
risotto, 64–65, 88–89
Roasted Corn & Apple Risotto,
    88–89
Roasted Pineapple Brûlée
    Donuts, 132–33
Roesti Benedict, 105
Romanesco, 146–48
Root Beer Schnapps, 122
Ropa Vieja, 199
Royal Pub Pizza, 81–82
rum, 119, 120, 123, 139

Saffron-Leek Cream Sauce,
    116–17

salads, 41–42, 52–53, 77
Salmorejo with Shrimp,
    Avocado & Serrano
    Ham, 56
salsas, 45
sandwiches, 24, 125–26
Sauce Meunière, 41–42
sauces, 8, 17, 18, 29–30, 34–35,
    40–41, 41–42, 45, 48, 51–52,
    60, 70, 81, 94, 97–98, 98,
    105, 107–8, 116, 119, 138–39,
    146–48, 148–49, 151, 155–56,
    162–63, 166–67, 175, 179, 181,
    189–90, 200–201
sauerkraut, 155–56
sausages, 51–52, 81–82, 142,
    143, 166–67
Sautéed Gulf Shrimp with
    Smoked Bacon & Cremini
    Mushroom Beurre
    Blanc, 175
Sautéed Lobster Tails, 74
scallops, 64–65, 70, 116–17, 159,
    162–63, 183
Scallops & Brie with Ruby Port
    Reduction, 159
Seafood Lasagna Trescaline,
    162–63
Seared Sea Scallops with
    Edamame, Roasted
    Shiitakes & Sherry Miso
    Butter, 183
Sex Addict, 113–14
shakes, 27
shellfish. See specific types of
    shellfish
shiitakes, 183
shrimp, 8, 9, 48, 51–52, 56, 71,
    94, 119, 162–63, 175, 177,
    189–90
Shrimp Bundles with Basil &
    Prosciutto, 9
Shrimp & Grits, 189–90
Shrimp Portofino Sauce, 48
Shrimp Sliders, 51–52

slaws, 45, 128, 187
Sloppy Joe's Mojito, 120
Smoked Bacon and Cremini
    Mushroom Beurre Blanc, 175
Smothered Tenderloin
    Medallions, 29–30
snapper, 17, 45, 67–68, 90,
    107–8
soups, 12, 14–15, 56
Soy-Lime Dressing, 110–11,
    128–29
Spicy Pub Conch Fritters, 82
spinach, 196
squash blossoms, 52–53
steak, 195
stews, 71, 142
Stormy Waters, 119
strawberries, 113–14
Sun-dried Tomato Relish, 151
Sunset Pier's Pusser's
    Painkiller, 139
sunset watching, 136
sushi, 37
Sweet Chili Sauce, 17
Sweet Corn Cream, 52–53
Sweet Potato Crusted Grouper
    with Truffle Cauliflower
    Puree and Roasted Garlic
    & Thyme Cream Sauce,
    146–48
sweet potatoes, 92–93,
    146–48, 200–201

tacos, 128–29
tagine, 165–66
tangerines, 90
tequila, 121
Tequila Ceviche Little Palm
    Island, 90
Thyme Cream Sauce, 146–47
tiradito, 37
Toasted Almond-Encrusted
    Grouper with Warm
    Caribbean Pineapple Relish,
    92–93

tomatillos, 181
tomatoes, 23, 41–42, 51–52,
    52–53, 56, 81–82, 107–8,
    135, 151, 177
Tomato-Fennel Sauce, 51–52
tostados, 181
Tropical Sauce, 60
Tropical Sweet Chili Salsa, 45
Truffle Cauliflower Puree,
    146–47
Truffled Creamed Spinach, 196
Truffle Vinaigrette, 41–42
tuna, 97–98, 110–11, 185
Tuna Tartare, 110–11

Vera Cruz Sauce, 119
vinaigrettes, 41–42, 67–68, 187

vodka, 160
Voodoo Seafood Stew, 71

wahoo, 90
walnuts, 171–72
Warm Caribbean Pineapple
    Relish, 92–93
Warm Vegetable Slaw, 45
wasabi, 97–98, 110–11
watermelon, 52–53
White Truffle Lobster Mac &
    Cheese, 31
Whole Fried Snapper with
    Tropical Sweet Chili Salsa &
    Warm Vegetable Slaw, 45

Whole Roasted Yellowtail
    with Asian Vegetables,
    Jasmine Rice & Ginger Soy
    Vinaigrette, 67–68
World Famous Hog's
    Breath Saloon Key
    Lime Shooter, 123

Yellowfin Tuna Ceviche, 185
yellowtail snapper, 17, 45,
    67–68, 90, 107–8
Yellowtail Snapper in Citrus
    Sauce, 107–8
Yellowtail Tiradito, 37
yellowtail tuna (hamachi), 37

About the Author

Far from the culture shock she expected upon moving to the Keys in 1993, Victoria Shearer discovered that island life opened the window on a tropical wonderland of sun, sea, and the sweeping bounty of Mother Nature. An avid traveler and no stranger to the wonders of the world, Vicki concluded that the Florida Keys reign in a class by themselves. So, like the Bahamians and Cubans who adopted the islands centuries before her, she stayed.

A University of Wisconsin graduate, Vicki wore several professional hats—elementary school teacher, advertising agency account executive, cooking magazine copy editor—before combining her passion for food and travel with her love of writing. She has written for many national magazines and newspapers and is author of ten editions of *Insiders' Guide to the Florida Keys & Key West* (Globe Pequot), as well as *Walking Places in New England* (2001), *It Happened in the Florida Keys* (Globe Pequot, 2008), *The Florida Keys Cookbook* (Globe Pequot, 2006, 2013), *Quick, Cheap Comfort Food* (2009), *Leftover Makeovers* (2010), *Make-Ahead Meals* (2011), and *Slow Cooker Classics from Around the World* (2011).

Vicki divides her time between Islamorada, in the Keys, and Wake Forest, North Carolina, where she lives with her husband, Bob. No day is complete without puttering in the kitchen, but she also loves to play bridge, needlepoint, and cheer on her beloved Carolina Hurricanes hockey team. And while the title of "author" and "cook" are quite nice, Vicki's most cherished monikers are "Mom" (Brian and Lisa, Kristen and John) and "Gram" (Christopher, Bethany, Bobby, Ashleigh, Leia, Nicholas, and Sammy).

About the Photographer

Michael Marrero is an award-winning photographer specializing in commercial, lifestyle, and food photography. He currently lives in Key West with his wife and two dogs and can usually be found relaxing on his front porch enjoying a cold beer with friends.